LIBRARY FUNDRAISING

MODELS
FOR
SUCCESS

Edited by
DWIGHT F. BURLINGAME
for the
Publications Committee of the
Fund Raising and Financial Development Section
Library Administration and Management Association

American Library Association
Chicago and London 1995

Cover design by Richmond Jones

Text design and composition by Dianne M. Rooney in Caslon 540 and Optima using QuarkXpress 3.3 for the Macintosh 7100/66

Printed on 50-pound Thor Antique, a pH-neutral stock, and bound in 10-point C1S cover stock by Malloy Lithographing, Inc.

The paper used in this publication meets the minimum requirements of American National Standard for Information Sciences—Permanence of Paper for Printed Library Materials, ANSI Z39.48-1992. ∞

Library of Congress Cataloging-in-Publication Data

Library fundraising : models for success / edited by Dwight Burlingame.
     p. cm.
   Includes bibliographical references (p.) and index.
   ISBN 0-8389-0657-5
   1. Library fund raising—United States.   I. Burlingame, Dwight.
Z683.2.U6L53   1995
021.8'3'0973—dc20   95-32665

DEC 1 0 2003

Printed in the United States of America.

99 98 97 96 95   5 4 3 2 1

Contents

Introduction

Fundraising has played a varied role in the history of American libraries, from a significant role in the early days of academic and private libraries open to the public to a minimal role for most public libraries during most of this century. (Notable exceptions to this observation include the New York Public Library.) Major changes in the environment in which libraries operate today—the rapid growth of information, increased costs for services and materials, and demands for additional services that often require seeking alternative funding sources—have caused libraries to consider private fundraising much more seriously.

Obtaining the financial resources necessary to accomplish the mission of an organization—whether governmental or private, non-profit or for-profit, local or state, national or international—seems to be an important part of the terrain in managing any organization in today's world. Libraries are no exception. Even a casual reading of the library press reveals the increased pressure to raise private dollars for library activities that were once thought to be either the responsibility of direct tax dollars, as in the case of public libraries, or indirect tax dollars, as in the case of public institutions of higher education. Even private college and university librarians often thought that student fees provided the dollars necessary to accomplish their mission. Suffice it to say that a new day has arrived and fundraising is now a part of the administration of virtually any library. The cases described in this book illustrate the growing trend to seek alternative ways to raise needed resources for the nation's libraries.

History

Libraries in early American colleges were supported by private gifts, and they were generally not open to the public. Another common type of early library was owned by a private citizen but made available for public use. According to Kaser (1980), probably no more than a dozen of such privately owned but publicly used libraries were in existence in 1762. Social or association libraries, however, were quite popular in colonial America. "Benjamin Franklin's launching of a subscription library in Philadelphia in 1731 served as a model for many other libraries in Europe and North America" (Burlingame 1994). Operating a library for profit, based primarily on receiving fees for borrowing books, is first credited to William Rind, who in 1762 opened a 150-book circulating library in Annapolis, Maryland (Kaser 1980).

Public support for financing a *public* library did not begin until 1833, when the Reverend Abiel Abbott persuaded citizens to support the Peterborough Town Library in New Hampshire (Clark 1992). Andrew Carnegie's philanthropy to over fifteen hundred communities across the United States was a major stimulus for public tax support of libraries. The shift from the subscription lending libraries of the 1700s to the mainly publicly supported public libraries of today took well over one hundred years.

Libraries began experiencing major budget reductions during the 1970s, but citizen efforts to reverse this trend were partially successful in the 1980s and the first half of the 1990s. Currently, however, the failure to pass local levies is still often reported in the library press. Clearly, the ability to obtain multiple sources of financial support, from both public and private sectors, appears to be an increasingly important requirement for directors of all libraries, but especially of public libraries. A library development program integrated within the total management system of the library can assist in increasing revenues from public as well as private sources.

The Need and Changing Environment

In a 1990 survey of library leaders, Durrance and Van Fleet (1992) identified five categories of changes that would affect public libraries in the 1990s. Three of these categories—adopting public relations and marketing strategies, planning to meet community needs, and fundraising—clearly indicate the need for library development programs. It is insufficient, however, to simply affirm the need for fundraising—an aggressive and organized activity, professionally managed, is required.

As more nonprofit institutions have been created (over one million to date, according to INDEPENDENT SECTOR estimates), and as more public sector organizations are seeking funding from nongovernmental sources, competition for private support has increased dramatically. In his seminal work on fundraising in university libraries, Andrew Eaton (1971) observed that most librarians did not consider fundraising part of their work and thus it had been a neglected part of librarianship. Eight years later, Breivik and Gibson (1979) noted that "most libraries seem reluctant to engage in major fund-raising efforts"(pp. 8–9). Even today, some libraries are still reluctant to become involved in major fundraising.

The cases contained in this book highlight the need for major fundraising efforts by libraries. Whether from individuals, foundations, or federal grants—the new and innovative, the special and extra service, and that which makes for excellence comprise the most appropriate purposes of soliciting private support. White (1992) captured this thought in his argument that the management structure must be held accountable for funding libraries adequately and that libraries are not charitable organizations. Jeffrey Krull (1991) also has warned that library fundraising should be used to "supplement, not supplant" (p. 65).

A Developing Field

Major changes have taken place since Eaton's observation in 1971. Not only do we have a vast array of how-to fundraising literature available (Hayes 1990) in the form of books, magazines, the *Chronicle of Philanthropy* newspaper, the New Directions series by Jossey-Bass entitled *Taking Fundraising Seriously*, and thousands of articles, but also we have the beginnings of a small and growing scholarly literature. Examples of this literature can be found in the *Nonprofit and Voluntary Sector Quarterly, Voluntas, Nonprofit Management and Leadership*, and the publications of the INDEPENDENT SECTOR research forums. In addition, a new index entitled *Philanthropic Studies Index* covers English language literature relevant to the nonprofit and voluntary sector, including much written on fundraising.

Over thirty academic and research centers for the study of the nonprofit sector have been formed in the United States over the last two decades, all of which are adding important contributions to the study and research in the field (Crowder and Hodgkinson 1991). The most comprehensive of these is the Center on Philanthropy, established at Indiana University in 1987. In 1993 an organization was formed—the International Society for Third-Sector Research (ISTR), which is an international and multidisciplinary scholarly association. Part of this association's purpose is to understand philanthropic behavior, which illustrates again the growing importance of fundraising as an academic subject.

Membership in professional fundraising associations has also grown significantly, with the three most visible being the Council for Advancement and Support of Education (CASE), the National Society for Fundraising Executives (NSFRE), and the Association for Healthcare Philanthropy (AHP). In addition, the Foundation Center's latest directory of funding sources for libraries and information services and the American Library Association's directory of granting sources illustrate the growing importance of fundraising in our lives.

Many professional organizations have added divisions or committees that deal exclusively with fundraising. In the 1980s, the Association of College and Research Libraries (ACRL) Fund Raising and Development Discussion Group, the Library Administration and Management Association (LAMA) Fund Raising and Financial Development Section, and the Public Library Association (PLA) Fund Raising Committee were established. In addition, a number of professional library development officers formed a group that is known today as Development Officers of Research Academic Libraries, North America, or DORAL, N.A.

A March 1992 SPEC survey of members of the Association of Research Libraries (ARL) showed that fundraising was a well-developed function in many research libraries (ARL 1993). Three other important studies of fundraising in libraries have been carried out under the auspices of the American Library Association over the last five years. *Non-Tax Sources of Revenue for Public Libraries* (Lynch 1988) found that likely sources of private support for libraries were individuals or Friends of Libraries groups. Only 14.9 percent of public libraries in this study reported no income obtained from fundraising (p. 2). The study concluded, however, that most libraries have not developed their private fundraising capabilities. A companion study, *Alternative Sources of Revenue in Academic Libraries,* found that the level of private fundraising was significant at higher educational institutions—particularly at those that granted doctorates (Lynch 1991, p. 2).

The LAMA Fund Raising and Financial Development Section conducted a survey of academic, public, and state libraries in 1985 (Fischler 1987; Burlingame 1987), then followed up with a survey of public libraries in 1989 (Burlingame 1990). In both studies, a majority of librarians felt that fundraising was important in meeting special needs and in gaining valuable support. Burlingame found that public libraries used book sales as the most common type of fundraiser and that the public relations function of fundraising activities was as important as the dollars raised. The role that volunteers and special events play in gaining public belief in the mission of the library and the subsequent confirmation of that belief by citizens voting for library levies needs to be studied further.

The genesis of this book was in discussions of the LAMA Fund Raising and Financial Development Section regarding surveys that the section as well as other groups had conducted in the mid-1980s of academic, public, and state libraries. Results of the surveys spurred these groups to enhance the literature with a series of case studies that would demonstrate not only fundraising successes, but also the pitfalls and how to avoid them.

As editor of this book, I have selected cases from a variety of libraries, and have tried to emphasize different fundraising approaches, including annual programs, special events, capital campaigns, and developing foundations and endowments.

Annual Campaigns

The first case in this book, submitted by Leland Park, director of E. H. Little Library, illustrates how the Davidson College's annual book gift program turned into an endowment, which is now a significant component of the library's resource base. This case illustrates the major components of a development program, with a particular emphasis on simple record keeping and thanking and recognizing donors.

Also illustrated in this case is how an academic library can and must find its particular niche within the total development program of the college or university. Being a team player with the central campus development office is an important rule for any librarian to keep in mind while planning for the library's fundraising efforts.

Capital Campaigns

Libraries often use capital campaigns for buildings to enlist private support. The Tufts University Wessell Library renovation case by

Murray S. Martin and the Chanute, Kansas, public library new building program case by James Swan illustrate a university and a small public library approach to expansion. Both approaches define elements, common to any size library, that are needed when building development programs and capital campaigns.

In both the Chanute and Tufts campaigns, the following items were key to the success of the projects:

1. A lead gift representing a significant portion of the total goal was obtained. Other major gifts represented the majority of the fundraising effort. In the Chanute case, nineteen contributors gave close to 70 percent of the funds for the entire project. This follows closely the 90/10 guideline that most expert fundraisers now suggest for fundraising campaigns; that is, 90 percent of the funds will come from 10 percent of the donors.
2. A clear vision of the project was communicated to the local community and leadership was provided.
3. The project had broad-based community support.

The Kansas project was assisted by Title II Library Services and Construction Act funds, as have many public library building projects. In other words, tax dollars were combined with private dollars to accomplish the goals of acquiring new physical quarters for the library. Was there a concern that private dollars would drive out public dollars in this case? By most indicators the answer is no. Rather, the central question seemed to be how sufficient funds—both private and public—could be obtained to accomplish the goals that had been set. The stark reality of limited tax revenues created positive and effective partnerships between local governmental officials and private funders to make the project successful.

Challenge Grants

Challenge grants have been and continue to be an important source to libraries for broadening their base of funding. The Johns Hopkins Library case by Kenneth E. Flower illustrates how one fundraising effort can lead to another, more ambitious effort. The importance of repeat giving and increasing the dollar amount of gifts are clearly illustrated.

This case illustrates the importance of recognizing that a library in an academic setting has an important story to tell and a constituency to whom to tell it. One often hears the refrain that academic libraries do not have natural constituencies. Obviously, the Hopkins Library as well as the Davidson Library did not let this perceived obstacle deter them from accomplishing their fundraising goals.

Foundations

The Atlanta-Fulton public library system case by Jennye E. Guy illustrates many of the political issues surrounding the development of a private arm of the library for raising money. In addition, it illustrates the importance of careful planning and the truth of the expression: "Don't give up."

Because of the concern to keep private and public support separate, a library foundation with its own governing body was created as the major vehicle for fundraising. Two library trustees and the library director formed the initial leadership of the foundation, which was a separate 501(c)(3) organization. As Jennye Guy, development officer of the library notes, the creation of the foundation was primarily done to assure donors that their gifts would not be "usurped" by government officials and that they would be used in the way the donors intended.

Grants from the state of Georgia and Fulton County (i.e., public revenues) were solicited in addition to private funds. A fundraising firm was retained to do a feasibility study, which determined that the library system had a mixed identity: the library had a low profile image among the public, and the public had a perception that the library did not need any private support because it was a governmental unit. The library addressed this issue with an aggressive public awareness program that was anchored around library branch construction projects, which had been made possible by an earlier referendum.

Being sure that potential donors know and believe in your cause is of great importance, as is illustrated by the Atlanta experience. Cultivation and more cultivation of donors is the rule. The goodwill created by public relations efforts had a direct bearing on the proposed budget cuts being reduced. In other words, the private fundraising effort translated into more support by government rather than less. This is an important observation in that it suggests that private fundraising in public libraries should not be viewed as a separate campaign. Rather, such efforts should be viewed and constructed as integral campaigns to raise public as well as private support for the library. For if support for the mission of the library is obtained from private citizens, this support may be translated into public support of the library by either additional taxes, increased share of the tax dollar, maintaining current levels of support, or not as great a cut in support that otherwise might have happened had not the public relations campaign been in place. Because of the multiple and complex variables that exist in communities, it is indeed difficult to say for certain that "x" action prevented "y". However, it is clear from many observations that the development effort averted reduction in service by the library.

From the perspective of the Atlanta-Fulton case study, one can conclude that change and flexibility are often needed when mounting campaigns. Most important, however, is the fact that the library was ultimately able to gain part of the philanthropic dollar without jeopardizing public support. In fact, seeking private support and gaining the knowledge of how to run a development program increased public support.

Using a vehicle such as a separate foundation appears to be more popular among public libraries. Most academic libraries use their institutional equivalent mechanisms. The foundation serves the multiple purposes of raising "friends," acquiring funds, and holding money (endowment) for the library. In most cases, the foundation's purpose is to enrich the basic services that the library provides with revenue from other sources.

Endowment Building

In the Tulsa Library Trust case, Cathy Audley and Pat Woodrum illustrate how dramatic growth in a library endowment was accomplished. This case clearly illustrates the importance of volunteer involvement and a sense of community.

In just ten years, the Tulsa Library Trust has grown in funding from under $14,000 to nearly $5,000,000. For the twentieth anniversary of the Tulsa City-County library system's establishment, the trust board and the library commission joined forces to develop the endowment. Part-time development functions were assigned to the library's public relations officer; this officer was to coordinate efforts with the library executive director and volunteers in planning and carrying out a campaign. Following good fundraising practice, their first step was conducting a feasibility study.

Because the volunteers on the trust board did not have the desired fundraising experience, a trust development committee was created, consisting of respected donors with expertise in fundraising in the community. After considerable research on potential donors, a campaign goal of $2 million was set. Consideration was given, then rejected, to employing outside counsel after it was determined that a low-key staff and a volunteer campaign were preferable.

A case statement was written that emphasized the enhancements that the interest gained from the endowment would provide to existing services provided by public funds. A public relations and marketing plan was then implemented involving hundreds of volunteers, and focusing on the library's role in the community. A concentrated effort to secure larger donations of $10,000 to $100,000 was made.

This case indicates how private dollars can complement public dollars when the vision of the library is meshed with the local and larger context. This shows how the economic, political, and social environments affect the library. The importance of having a clear case statement and a blueprint for action built on solid research echoes throughout this case.

In the final case study, Victoria Steele emphasizes the importance of a partnership between the librarian and the development officer. This is of particular importance for organizations that need to work with a central development office, as is the case in most colleges and universities. Understanding each other's role in the fundraising process and having a clear understanding of what development people expect from librarians and what librarians expect from development personnel will go a long way to producing an effective development team.

Utilizing the example of the Scripter Award special events program, Steele illustrates how the respective roles of the special collections librarian and the development officer are put into action, and how the event can succeed or fail. The reader is left with a recognition that fundraising is often an art that needs the guidance of the expert fundraiser and the commitment of the librarian (student of fundraising). Working together, they create a successful program.

Librarians, fundraisers, volunteers, and students of libraries should find this book useful. The stories within provide many ideas for potential implementation and important ideas for thoughtful reflection. Happy reading.

DWIGHT BURLINGAME

Notes

Association of Research Libraries. 1993. *Library development and fundraising: A SPEC kit.* Washington, D.C.: Association of Research Libraries, Office of Management Services.

Breivik, P. S. and E. B. Gibson, eds. 1979. *Funding alternatives for libraries.* Chicago: American Library Association.

Burlingame, D. F. 1991. Fund raising and financial development. In J. Lester, ed., *Libraries and information services today,* 111–14. Chicago: American Library Association.

_____. 1994. Fund-raising as a key to the library's future. *Library Trends* 42(3): 467–77.

_____. (1987). Library fund-raising in the United States: A second look. *Library Administration & Management* 1(3): 108–11.

_____. 1990. Public libraries and fundraising: Not-so-strange bedfellows. *Library Journal* 115(12): 52–54.

Clark, C. S. 1992. Hard times for libraries. (issue theme) *CQ Researcher* 2(24): 549–71.

Crowder, N. L. and V. A. Hodgkinson, eds. 1991. *Compendium of resources for teaching about the nonprofit sector, voluntarism and philanthropy.* Washington, D.C.: INDEPENDENT SECTOR.

Durrance, J. and C. Van Fleet. 1992. Public libraries: Adapting to change. *Wilson Library Bulletin* 67(2): 30–35, 117–18.

Eaton, A. J. 1971. Fund raising for university libraries. *College & Research Libraries* 32(5): 351–61.

Fischler, B. F. 1987. Library fund-raising in the United States: A preliminary report. *Library Administration & Management* 1(1): 31–34.

Harr, B. 1994. Crossing the line: Raising funds for public libraries. *Advancing Philanthropy* 2(2): 38–40.

Hayes, S. 1990. Fund raising: A brief bibliography In D. F. Burlingame, ed., *Library development: A future imperative,* 135–52. Binghamton, N.Y.: Haworth.

Kaser, David. 1980. *A book for a sixpence: The circulating library in America.* Pittsburgh: Beta Phi Mu.

Krull, J. R. 1991. Private dollars for public libraries. *Library Journal* 116(1): 65–68.

Lynch, M. J. 1991. *Alternative sources of revenue in academic libraries.* Chicago: American Library Association, Office for Research.

_____. 1988. *Non-tax sources of revenue for public libraries.* Chicago: American Library Association, Office for Research.

White, H. S. 1992. Seeking outside funding: The right and wrong reasons. *Library Journal* 117(12): 48–49.

1 Endowed Book Funds

A Million Dollars, Step-by-Step, for a Small College Library

LELAND M. PARK

Receiving a million dollar check to endow the purchase of books at a small college library would be wonderful, but the chances of it happening are remote for most institutions. Slowly building a million dollar endowment for books, however, in a small college library is *not* a remote possibility. It can be done.

At Davidson College the library staff is small, and the time available to the library director for raising money is a small amount. But the library's need to raise funds for an endowment is very real. Because the college is located in a non-urban area of the state, a Friends group, organized along traditional lines, was not really a possibility. The only members who would attend meetings would be the same people who attend everything else on campus, and the opportunity to reach out to others not in the college community was limited. In addition, staff in charge of development activities for the college-at-large discouraged the library from going after smaller gifts because their office might be contacting the same people for substantial gifts. The library did not want to be in competition with other college departments; rather, it wanted to complement their activities.

In 1956, an alumnus donated $57,000 to the college for the library in memory of his mother. The college set up a line item in

Leland Park is the director of E. H. Little Library at Davidson College, North Carolina.

the budget and the income from the donation was used to purchase books. Fifteen years later, the parents of an alumnus who died in Vietnam donated in his memory $1,000 to endow the purchase of an annual update for a serial set. At that time, library staff then decided that this method of raising funds for the library was appropriate and should be organized and pursued. It was felt the funds could grow significantly over time. And they have.

The fundraising plan is a simple one. It is based on the following assumptions:

1. People have warm feelings about a library because of their personal experiences as well as their perceptions about what a library does.
2. Some people need lower-dollar donation targets in addition to larger-dollar opportunities, such as buildings, collections, and so on.
3. People like to have a "receipt" for their gift, to be reminded regularly of their gift's value and what it meant to the recipient.
4. The staff administering the fundraising program is small and thus the program should be simply devised.
5. The library will need the help of others to "spread the word" to help solicit funds.

Elements of the Program

Financial Procedures

For every $500 donated, the library promises to acquire one book per year in the name of the book fund. All of the funds are "open ended" and may be added to at any time. For example, a gift of $1,500 permits three books to be purchased annually by that fund. If donors later add $1,000 to the fund, the library will purchase five books per year in the name of that fund.

The funds are deposited with the controller's office, which then adds the funds to the college endowment funds, which are administered by the college's investment service. A separate line item in the college budget is maintained for each fund, indicating the initial dollar value plus any funds subsequently added to the fund during the fiscal year. The college annually totals the dollar value of all of these funds. The library can use 5 percent of the total funds (i.e., $25 per $500) to spend for books over the next fiscal year. If the endowment earns more than this amount (e.g., 8 percent), the excess is added to the endowment.

Note that whereas the controller's office keeps separate books on each fund, the income from *all* of the funds is consolidated and given to the library as one line item in its material budget. No effort is made to ensure that the exact amount each fund earns is spent for books—the bookkeeping required would be outrageous. The library promised one book per year per $500 of principal; it did *not* promise to spend the exact amount on one particular book. This simplifies the procedures considerably.

The library now has a line item in its material budget for "endowed funds." That amount, whatever it is, is spent to pay invoices for books. No effort is made to match the invoices for endowed fund books with actual books that are labeled for the funds. That, too, would be a difficult and unnecessary task. A library will always (unless it is unusually fortunate) buy more books than the endowment produces, so it does not matter which dollars pay for which book. Once that line item is spent for the year, the matter is closed financially.

Designation Procedures

The library business manager keeps a list of all funds contributed along with the amount of principal in each fund as of the thirtieth of June of each year. That figure is obtained from the controller's annual audited report. The list is kept on the library computer and is easily updated. Based on one book purchased per $500 of principal, the business manager then notes how many units (books) each fund produces per year. Also noted is any book subject area to which a fund is limited. That list—names of funds, amounts of principal, number of units, subject areas—is then given to the acquisitions manager.

The acquisitions manager has a 3" x 5" card file with dividers listing each fund, and into that card file the number of bookplates needed that year for each fund is placed. For instance, if Fund A has a principal of $3,500, then seven bookplates are placed in back of the divider for Fund A. On the divider is written any subject area to which the fund is limited. Figure 1.1 shows the information fields on a card.

During the course of the year as the acquisitions manager is checking in book orders, he or she will place bookplates from the various book funds in individual books, thereby designating those

Name of Fund:
    DC Class of Honoree:
    Other DC Connections:

Date Established (Mo/Yr):
Donor(s):   DC Class:
    Other DC Connections:
    Address:
    Address of Others to Be Kept Posted of Fund:

Relationship of Donor to Honoree:
Subject Area Books Are to Be Selected:
Initial Value of Fund:

Present Value of Fund (List Amount and Date):
On reverse, please list donors to fund other than initiator of fund.

Figure 1.1   Endowed Fund Record Form

books as a gift of Fund A. When the book is received in the cataloging department, the bookplate is pasted inside the front cover of the book. When an endowed fund book is cataloged, the author and title are listed under the fund name in a computer file so that a running record of books in that fund is kept. The book continues on the regular processing route and no other disruption to the processing schedule is experienced by either department.

Bookplates

The college relations office is in charge of publications for the college. Through that office the library has established a standard format for bookplates, each the same size and with the same basic wording. When a fund is initiated, the bookplate wording is established by the library director, usually in collaboration with the donor, and the business manager arranges for bookplates to be printed. Each summer the supply is replenished when all library printing supplies are handled. Figure 1.2 shows sample bookplates.

Donor Recognition

People usually enjoy giving to a college and particularly to a library. Donors understandably like to have some acknowledgment of their

Figure 1.2   Sample Bookplates. Used with permission

gift, a recognition that the gift was used for something lasting. The endowed book funds offer this type of recognition. For example:

The library director acknowledges gifts with a careful explanation of the value of such funds, noting that they are all "open-ended" funds.

In a conference room in the library are blank frames hanging on the walls in which are placed one bookplate for each book fund with the year of its establishment noted. The donors therefore have a visual acknowledgment of their gift that they can see when they are on campus.

Small 3" x 5" frames, which can be hung on the wall or stood up on a desk or table, are purchased from a framing shop. A copy of the bookplate is placed in one of these and given to the donor and the honoree, if appropriate. This is used as a thank-you gift as well as a gentle reminder that "their fund" is still out there.

In the college catalog are various lists for endowed scholarships, awards, *and* endowed book funds. A two- or three-line entry for each fund indicates its name, the donor, the honoree, and any relatives of the donor or honoree who have attended Davidson (see Figure 1.3).

Two or three times a year, a Library Friends List is published in the format of a newsletter. See Figure 1.4 for an excerpt. Each fund that has purchased books for the collection during that period is listed, along with titles the fund has purchased. If the fund has purchased more than four books during that period, the four titles are listed, followed by the words "and x others." (To do otherwise, once many funds have been established, would require exorbitant postage costs.) The list is maintained in a computer file in the cataloging department. When the time comes for publishing the newsletter, the library director reviews the list, and the college relations office sets the type for the newsletter. Copies of the newsletter are sent to each donor and honoree, if appropriate. Also, copies are placed in every faculty and staff mailbox, and are sent to members of the Board of Trustees, Board of Visitors, and directors of other libraries.

When the controller's annual audit is published, the library director writes to each donor, enclosing a copy of the section of the annual report showing the financial data about the donor's fund as well as a copy of the listing of the fund in the college catalog. These items, along with a letter about library events, are a continuation of library contact with the donor and a gentle reminder that the funds are "open ended."

Christmas cards from library staff—usually a calendar for the year with the library's name, address, and phone number— are sent to donors each year.

Occasionally, other published items are sent to donors during the year.

Because the donor list is kept in a computer file, addressing envelopes for these mailings is a routine task.

ENDOWED BOOK FUNDS

The income from these funds established by family and friends of the honorees, is used to purchase books for the library each year. All of the funds are open-ended. The total of all endowed book funds in the library is now more than $1,200,000.

The Jean Elizabeth Alexander Fund — Established by members of the Hawley Memorial Presbyterian Church, Polkton, N.C.

The Atwell Alexander and Pauline Hill Alexander Fund — Established by Mr. and Mrs. Alexander, Stony Point, North Carolina. Mr. Alexander is a 1929 Davidson graduate.

The Alumni Association/Wildcat Club Fund — Established by a gift from these two Davidson organizations.

The Alumni Travel Fund — Established by participants in travel programs sponsored by the Alumni Association.

The Nancy Rodden Arnette Fund — Established by family and friends in memory of the Administrative Secretary to the Vice President for Academic Affairs, 1974-1985.

The Joseph Abrams Bailey Fund — Established by his daughter, Mrs. Helen Bailey Obering of Oklahoma City. Mr. Bailey, a native of Clinton, South Carolina, was a member of the Class of 1883.

The Carrie Harper Barnhardt Fund — Established by Davidson Trustee and Mrs. James H. Barnhardt of Charlotte, North Carolina, in memory of his mother.

The Deborah Kinley Barnhardt Fund — Established by Davidson Trustee and Mrs. James H. Barnhardt, Sr. in honor of their daughter-in-law, Mrs. Sadler H. Barnhardt of Charlotte, North Carolina.

The Dorothy McDougle Barnhardt Fund — Established by Davidson Trustee and Mrs. James H. Barnhardt, Sr. in honor of their daughter-in-law, Mrs. James H. Barnhardt, Jr., of Charlotte, North Carolina

The James H. Barnhardt Fund — Established in honor of Davidson Trustee Barnhardt by Dr. Warner L. Hall, Chairman-emeritus of the Davidson Board of Trustees.

The Mr. and Mrs. Thomas M. Barnhardt Fund — Established by their children.

The Lucille Hunter Beall Fund — Established by McPherson Scott Beall '25, in memory of his wife.

The Mary Davis Beaty Fund — Established by family and friends in memory of Dr. Beaty, Assistant Director and Reference Coordinator of the E.H. Little Library, 1973-1992.

The Robert B. Bennett, Jr. Endowed Fund — Established by Robert B. Bennett, Jr., Class of 1977.

The Thomas M. Bernhardt Fund — Established by family and friends of this 1974 graduate, Director of the Living Endowment from 1975-1978.

The Anna Augusta Sutton Bledsoe Fund — Established by Dana Professor of History Emeritus Malcolm Lester in memory of his grandmother.

The Francis Marion Bledsoe, M.D. Fund — Established by Dana Professor of History Emeritus Malcolm Lester in memory of his grandfather.

The David B. Bostian, Sr. Fund — Established by David B. Bostian, Jr. '64 and Mrs. Clara K. Bostian.

The Royal L. Branton Fund — Established by W. Coleman Branton '36 in memory of his brother, a 1941 graduate.

The William Coleman Branton Fund — Established in memory of this member of the Class of 1936 by his wife.

The Herman Spencer Caldwell, Sr. and Richard Earl Caldwell Fund — Established by family and friends of Herman S. '33 and Richard E. '37. Herman S., Jr. is a 1967 graduate.

Figure 1.3   College Catalog Excerpt. Used with permission

LIBRARY NEWSLETTER

NUMBER 3, MAY 1994

RECENT GIFTS FROM FRIENDS OF THE DAVIDSON COLLEGE LIBRARY

DR. ANTHONY S. ABBOTT
  A Small Thing Like a Breath
    Authored by donor

MR. & MRS. THOMAS W. ABELL
  Global Accord

DR. GEORGE L. ABERNETHY
  The Best of Charles Dana Gibson
  Painting and Sculpture in the Museum of
    Modern Art
  Raphael Soyer Drawings and Watercolors

THE ATWELL ALEXANDER (1929) AND
PAULINE HILL ALEXANDER FUND
  Religious Holidays and Calendars
  Stravinsky
  Women Playwrights
  Plus 18 other vols.

MRS. J. W. ALEXANDER
in memory of Mr. Hugh D. Cashion, Sr. (1933)
  The Power "To Coin" Money

DR. JAMES M. ALEXANDER
in honor of Mrs. Frances Overcash
  Biomedical Engineering

THE JEAN ELIZABETH ALEXANDER FUND
  Children in the House

THE ALUMNI ASSOCIATION AND
THE WILDCAT CLUB FUND
  Egypt

THE ALUMNI TRAVEL BOOK FUND
  Dispatches from the Pacific Century
  In the Footsteps of Genghis Khan

THE NANCY RODDEN ARNETTE FUND
  The Antilles
  Reading Shakespeare's Characters
  Superfluous Things

THE JOSEPH ABRAMS BAILEY (1883) FUND
  Shakespeare on Screen
  Watteau's Painted Conversation
  Voices from the Holocaust
  Plus 293 other vols.

MR. JOSEPH TODD BAILEY (1980)
  Looking Homeward

DR. RUPERT T. BARBER, JR.
  Soliloquy! the Shakespeare Monologues

DR. BEN DALE BARKER (1954)
  The Oxford English Dictionary 2nd Ed.
    (20 vols.)

THE CARRIE HARPER BARNHARDT FUND
  The Man Who Stayed Behind

THE DEBORAH KINLEY BARNHARDT FUND
  Max Weber and the Jewish Question

THE DOROTHY McDOUGLE BARNHARDT FUND
  On Our Own Ground

THE JAMES H. BARNHARDT FUND
  Chronicle of Aviation
  Galileo Courtier
  The World's Emerging Stock Markets

THE MR. AND MRS. THOMAS M.
BARNHARDT FUND
  The Bridges of Madison County
  B. F. Skinner
  Navajo Aging
  Plus 23 other vols.

THE LUCILLE HUNTER BEALL FUND
  The Batak
  Indian Country, L. A.
  The Spy Who Saved the World
  Plus 6 other vols.

THE MARY DAVIS BEATY FUND
  The Age of Grace
  Have a Nice Day - No Problem!
  A Life in Music
  Plus 11 other vols.

THE ROBERT BERNARD BENNETT, JR. (1977)
FUND
  The Aztecs
  Cicero and the Roman Republic

DR. & MRS. RICHARD R. BERNARD
  The Original Water-Color Paintings
    by John James Audubon

THE THOMAS M. BERNHARDT (1974) FUND
  Ernest Hemingway
  The Rock Art of Easter Island
  Wordsworth
  Plus 3 other vols.

MR. LESLIE G. BERRY, JR.
  Aurora Leigh

THE ANNA AUGUSTA SUTTON BLEDSOE FUND
  James Branch Cabell and
    Richmond-in-Virginia

THE FRANCIS MARION BLEDSOE FUND
  The Wounded River

THE DAVID B. BOSTIAN, SR. FUND
  Schumann: Fantasie, Op. 17

THE WILLIAM COLEMAN BRANTON (1936)
FUND
  The Inner Ocean
  Institutions for the Earth
  Losing Time

DR. E. E. BROWN (1928)
  Bankruptcy 1995
  Inside American Education
  Sarapiqui Chronicle

THE HERMAN SPENCER CALDWELL, SR.
(1933) AND RICHARD EARL CALDWELL
(1937) FUND
  Battle for the Elephants
  Fourier Transform Infrared
  Guide to the Liverworts of North Carolina
  Handbook of Current Science
    & Technology

THE LILLIE HALTIWANGER CALDWELL FUND
  Brain Development and Cognition
  Friendship and Peer Relations in Children
  Learning To be Modern
  Learning Together

THE PRESTON BANKS CARWILE (1920) FUND
  The Evolution of Mozart's Pianistic Style

THE HUGH D. CASHION, SR. (1933) FUND
  The Way of the Pipa

DR. LARRY S. CHAMPION (1954)
  The Essential Shakespeare
    Authored by donor (Davidsoniana Room)

MR. J. W. NELSON CHANDLER (1997)
  History of Williamsburg Church
  Indiantown Presbyterian Church 1757-1957
  The Witherspoon Family Chronicle

Figure 1.4   Library Newsletter Excerpt. Used with permission

All of these items, none of which take a great deal of staff time, offer the donor regular feedback from the library and a reminder of the library's appreciation for the donor's support.

Publicizing the Funds

When the decision was made twenty years ago to establish endowed book funds, a simple brochure was printed explaining "the gift which keeps on giving." These brochures were given to every staff and faculty member on campus. Since then, the library director regularly mentions the establishment of new funds via development office publications that are sent to alumni and friends of the college. The library director takes every opportunity to discuss the funds with others on campus. Blind copies of thank-you notes to donors are sent to various administrative officers on campus as a way of keeping them posted as well as reminding them of this gift opportunity. Over time, endowed book funds are remembered by others as a possibility for donors. And over the years, the idea has taken hold.

Examples of Funds

Deceased faculty and staff members are often remembered "in lieu of flowers" with memorial gifts to the library. If the amount of a gift totals at least $500, the library director suggests to the family that the funds be used to establish an endowed book fund. The suggestion has never been declined, for it is a special way to remember the deceased. It is not unusual for the obituary notice in the newspaper to list an endowed book fund as an appropriate way to remember the deceased. Seventy percent of the funds have been given in memory of a friend, family member, or colleague.

Several funds have been established in honor of a living person. One student recently established two funds, each producing one book per year, in honor of two professors who made a special contribution to his life at Davidson. The chairman of the Board of Trustees established a fund in honor of a longtime friend in a nearby city. A faculty member, active on the library committee, established a fund honoring her grandmother, now in a retirement home. A family long connected with the college named a fund in honor of one of their siblings as a thank you for work he did for the family in handling a deceased family member's estate. A man and his two sons, all Davidson graduates, decided that an endowed book fund would be their "project" for Davidson. Regular gifts to the fund are received from each of them. A small foundation in Virginia wanted to honor a retiring attorney at his alma mater. He loves to collect books. A call to the library director for ideas resulted in a handsome endowed book fund, one to which the honoree has since contributed. A dentist, loyal to his alma mater, wanted a way to give to Davidson a quarterly remuneration he received for editing a professional newsletter. His love for the library led him to establish a fund with his name on it. About 20 percent of the funds are named in honor of someone. Over 10 percent of the funds are named for the donor.

Organizations have also established funds. One fraternity on campus decided its service project would be the establishment and support of an endowed book fund. The group publishes an annual activities calendar, listing all campus events for the year. Patron gifts are received and advertising is sold. The calendar is then sold on campus and in the town. After a decade of work, the Sigma Alpha Epsilon fraternity endowed book fund now totals over $50,000. One church, desiring to honor one of its members who had distinguished herself professionally, established a fund in her name. A church in a neighboring city raised money for the college. It indicated that the gift should go for scholarships *and* the library. An endowed book fund was established in its name.

Donors

Funds have been established by alumni, college faculty, college staff members, family and friends, and organizations. Alumni are the source for over 40 percent of the funds, whereas family and friends represent about 30 percent. College employees and groups or organizations each represent about 10 percent each of the total number of donors. Figure 1.5 summarizes the sources and honorees of funds.

A. Source of Funds	
Alumni	49%
College employees	11%
Family/friends	31%
Groups/organizations	9%
	100%
B. Honorees of Funds	
Donors	11%
In honor of	19%
In memory of	70%
	100%

Figure 1.5   Source of Endowed Funds and Honorees of Funds

Alternative Methods

Whereas cash gifts are appreciated, gifts designated for the future—planned giving—are also appreciated. To date, there have been ten bequests, some of which have already been received; others are expected at the time of the death of the donor (these, when received, are established exactly as the others). Some donors have their checking accounts debited for a monthly or quarterly gift through the development office.

Results

The development of the "family of funds" has been a slow, steady one. Ten were established in the 1970s, eighty were established in the 1980s, and approximately twenty-five have been established in the 1990s. The total monies in all the endowed book funds have grown from $57,000 in 1957 to over $1,300,000 in June of 1993. Figure 1.6 shows the duties of staff related to the fund.

What does this mean to the library and the college?

There is a new and growing source of income for the college library, amounting to about $65,000 per year.

The library is a beneficiary of "restricted money" that may be used only for the purchase of library materials. This money is guaranteed; it cannot be used for overhead or any other purpose. This will guarantee approximately 2,600 new books per year.

Staff Member	Duties
Library Director	Establish program
	Coordinate publicity
	Correspond with donors/honorees
	Arrange printing of Library Friends List
	Prepare list of funds for college catalog
Director's Secretary	Maintain files on each fund
	Coordinate mailings of Library Friends List
	Address Christmas cards to donors
Library Business Manager	Receive funds from director
	Establish accounts with controller
	Prepare chart of funds annually
	Prepare/stock bookplates
Acquisitions Manager	Select titles for each fund from those books received
Cataloging Staff Member	Paste label in book
	Keep list of funds and books purchased
	Prepare Library Friends List data for printer

Figure 1.6   Staff Duties Regarding Funds

Final Observations

An endowed book fund program takes time and organization to establish; however, once it is established, it almost maintains itself. Many staff members are involved, yet the burden on each one is not great. All feel they are making a substantial contribution toward the well-being of the library, its operation, and its future. And they are.

2 Tufts University— Wessell Library Renovations

MURRAY S. MARTIN

Capital projects for a library are both essential and difficult to fund. The need for such projects is clear, but the benefits are diffuse. The library has no alumni constituency and few ready supporters in the administration, which is probably more concerned about tuition costs and student loans. As a fundraiser once said to the author, "Libraries are not sexy." Since universities and colleges do not provide for depreciation or amortization of capital, they almost always rely on external funds for the replacement or modernization of buildings. Academic institutions usually have a long list of needs for such expenditure, so that the library must be prepared to compete with other units seeking new buildings. The first step in securing funding for a library's capital project, therefore, is to make the library's case compelling. The second is to demonstrate that it will be possible to raise the needed funds.

Preparation

Over the course of a university's lifetime, its library can be expected to grow and to require either a new building, a significant expansion, or internal renovations. In the case of Tufts University, the Wessell Library, built in 1964, had served its users well for twenty

Murray S. Martin is university librarian emeritus of Tufts University.

years but was becoming difficult to use effectively. Although it had some innovative features such as an audiovisual center and well-placed reading and study areas, it had originally been conceived as an undergraduate library and originally designed to serve the teaching needs of the college. The university had branch libraries for chemistry, physics, and engineering, so the principal users of Wessell Library were students from liberal arts, education, and the life sciences. Although added electrical wiring had been proposed at the time the library was planned, shortage of funds had caused most of it to be eliminated. The furniture and other fittings were custom designed, making it difficult to match the existing decor.

The library was also showing signs of age and the academic environment had changed—more graduate programs, a higher student enrollment, and higher library expectations. Combining these facts into a fundraising statement meant a lot of work. Whereas the needs may be self-evident to a librarian, they are not so obvious to administrators and fundraisers, who have many other priorities. Libraries are less likely to attract funds than computers or art galleries. This may mean, in fundraising terms, that any major project has to be divided into sellable parts, some of which will attract money readily, while others will simply have to be folded into general construction.

Preparatory Work

By 1986 the groundwork for a major project at Wessell Library had been laid through documenting the need for the work in annual reports and position papers. It is impossible to overstate the importance of demonstrating need, particularly in a time when general finances are short. In this case, the need to make the library capable of taking advantage of new electronic technologies was emphasized. The important concern here was to express the need by stressing the positive effects rather than negative ideas such as: the library was too small, there was no space to carry out ordinary activities, and so on. Instead, improvements for users were emphasized: better access to electronic information, better working conditions, and better access to materials. Given that the Wessell Library was also a campus landmark, describing the renovation project as restoring the library's image rather than correcting its deficiencies was an important consideration. In addition, care was given to emphasize the ways in which donors could be associated with an important component of academic life. Wherever possible, attention was drawn to the extended possibilities of electronic information transfer, a sign that the library was part of the new age in education, rather than a symbol of the past. This aspect of need was important in attracting donations for innovative services.

In addition to laying the groundwork, the library had already instituted a number of smaller physical improvements whose positive impact on faculty and students had been noted. Based on this history, the university librarian put together a needs assessment, which was reviewed by the appropriate university officers. This assessment included both physical plant and operational improvements, stressing the ways in which a new library could improve service to students and faculty. Since the university was already considering ways in which it could use telecommunications to improve learning, it was crucial to show that the library could be a part of this change.

Needs Assessment

A general renovation program was outlined. It included:

Upgrading existing space to improve user service

Expanding and completing renovation of the audiovisual area, already heavily used

Better work areas for technical services, to improve productivity

Better work space for circulation and reserve staff and services, to improve library responsiveness

Total rearrangement of the reference area to house the online catalog and database services (the latter were then housed in what had been a typing room, some distance from the main reference area), to make these services more responsive to user needs

Expansion and renovation of the government documents and maps room, to make the materials accessible.

Preliminary estimates from the buildings and grounds department suggested a total expenditure of about $800,000. A small part of this could come from the annual library budget, as substitutional expenditure from line items for equipment and repairs, or from salary savings, but the largest part would have to come from outside sources. Review by the university officers resulted in a qualified approval, with the requirement that the library raise the necessary money. The College of Arts and Sciences would provide some funds from capital reserves, but could not finance the whole project. Support from the college's budget officer was crucial for the success of the project, and required a series of sessions refining the details.

Two years earlier an alumna, also a member of the library Board of Visitors, had agreed to fund a partial renovation of the audiovisual area, and the Booth-Ferris Foundation provided matching funds. The total for that renovation reached $150,000. This was taken as evidence that the library was an attractive fundraising project.

Finally, the library was just completing a major automation project, funded by a $500,000 grant from the Pew Charitable Trust, and foresaw the need for a local area network (LAN) to realize the full benefits of automation. The grant showed that the library was able to attract external support, and the proposal for a LAN was supported by the computer center, both crucial elements in gaining approval. While plans were being developed, it was determined that the roof of the building was in a serious state of disrepair. In addition, the university insurers had presented an ultimatum—install a sprinkler system or see the rates for insurance soar. As part of that project it was also determined that fire protection in the special collections area was inadequate, and should include a halon gas protection system. Both building needs were urgent, which provided an impetus to proceed immediately with the proposed renovations, with the condition that disruption to users be kept to a minimum.

Fundraising

With these background facts in mind, the library began to seek major funding for renovations, working through the development office, the sole university agency authorized to seek external funds. The university had already agreed that a major expansion of the library would be a part of the next capital campaign. Whereas the two projects could have been in conflict, a compromise was negotiated that allowed the library to seek funds for renovations that could be seen as leading to the larger project for an addition. For example, no actual construction would be undertaken that would have to be torn down later. These conditions meant that certain kinds of renovations would have to be postponed, but the library administration decided that it was better to proceed than to wait for a larger project. The library renovation was folded into the first stage of the capital campaign. This meant deciding which donors were interested in the library, what competition there was, and what impact immediate gifts would have on long-term campaign goals. The possibility of sequential gifts is a major concern of all development offices.

Discussions with development office staff soon focused on an approach to the Kresge Foundation, which had a history of funding library construction. The university was also interested in establishing a track record with this foundation. The Kresge Foundation required both a significant institutional effort to match funds (i.e., a foundation-to-institution dollar ratio of one-to-two) and that actual construction costs meet or exceed the amount from the foundation (in this case the final grant was $300,000). After a series of meetings, approval was given to approach the Kresge Foundation. This, of course, required detailed plans, so that buildings and grounds officers met with the architects and engineers who were planning the installation of the sprinkler system. The sprinkler system installation eventually required the replacement of the entire ceiling and all exposed electrical wiring. By meshing the renovation plans with the plans for the sprinkler system, total costs could be reduced. The installation would also match the new internal configurations.

Approval was given by the Kresge Foundation in 1986. The foundation was pleased to come in on a project in progress, since the work already undertaken showed a commitment, and because their challenge program was calculated to spur other donors to assist in completion. These factors complemented the goals of the larger capital campaign. The earlier partial renovation of the audiovisual area, funded by a grant of $75,000 from the Booth-Ferris Foundation and a similar amount from an alumna, provided evidence that the university was both serious in its intentions and able to attract funds. In the long run, foundation funding would provide only one-fifth of the total, since other factors such as the installation of the sprinkler system added to the total cost.

At this stage, finding the remainder of the funding was up to the development office staff. With the university librarian's assistance, donors were found. Several smaller grants were received from other foundations, from individuals, trustees and alumni, and unassigned general start-up funds from the capital campaign. Here the most important factor was the interest of the president of the university, who had the right of disposal on such donations.

The first need was to identify matching funds for the Kresge grant of $300,000. The university was required to find an additional $665,000. Part of this came from capital funds that were set aside by the College of Arts and Sciences, part came from trustee gifts to the capital campaign, and the rest came from smaller individual gifts. The university set aside money from maintenance reserves for roof repair, and part of a bond issue was used to meet the costs of the new sprinkler system. One condition imposed was that, wherever possible, grants and gifts should be substituted for university dollars. The total cost of the project over four years was more than $2 million. A substantial proportion of this was from external sources—over $1.3 million, including the bond issue. Several donors provided undesignated funds, but some asked for naming opportunities. In the long run, however, many parts of the project simply combined funding sources because it was too difficult to separate out nameable gifts.

Project Costs

A breakdown of project costs, excluding the installation of the sprinkler system and the new ceiling, shows the major expenditures:

Kresge-related projects:

Audiovisual expansion	$ 132,000
Public services renovations	89,500
Summer construction (documents and rare books)	245,423
Shelving	27,684
Roof	306,766
Subtotal	801,373
LAN	252,812
Total	$1,054,185

The costs were such that the university would have to find at least another $100,000 beyond the funds from the Kresge Foundation and the matching funds needed. The list also illustrates one of the other problems associated with project bookkeeping. Accounts had to be kept in accordance with project budgets, and it was not always clear what was covered by each project, since these were controlled by the buildings and grounds staff. The actual sources of the funds were unimportant to them, but essential for central accounting, development, and the library. At the end of the total project, reconciliation of the various figures reported in each set of accounts took more than a month because of the need to reconcile discrepancies between the various reports. Monthly, and toward the end of the project, weekly budget meetings were necessary. The staff costs involved were substantial and do not show up in the project budgets. A conservative estimate of the staff costs would be roughly 10 percent of the total, or about $100,000. These costs are seldom taken into account when setting out on a project, but mount rapidly.

The Project

Project difficulties arose because three different contractors were involved, working from plans drawn up at different stages of the process. In one area the whole lighting and sprinkler system had to be redesigned because the layout of the room concerned had changed. Nevertheless, the project was completed on time and within budget. This was quite an accomplishment, given the range of work and the time it took. The entire project required over four years to complete, largely because major work could only be done over the summer session and academic term breaks. The project was broken down into component parts, both to meet the requirements of the Kresge Foundation and because specific funding had been given for separate parts. There were only two specifically named parts—the new reference area and a meeting room—but others were constrained by the actual size of the donations being used. For example, the Surdna Foundation grant for technological renovations could only be used for the LAN, and the gift from the class of '35, while unassigned, was supposed to be used only for expenditures that could not be met from the regular budget. That proviso was met by using the funds to buy special equipment.

To summarize, the project included:

A new addition to audiovisual services—personal donation and Kresge grant

Shifting stack areas—library budget

Renovation of the reference area—alumna donor

Roof repairs—university maintenance funds and Kresge grant

Sprinkler system and electrical wiring replacements—university bond issue

LAN installation—Surdna grant and class gift

Renovation of circulation—capital funds

Relocation of microforms—Kresge grant

Relocation of current periodicals—Kresge grant

Relocation of fine arts—library funds

Redesign of government publications—capital funds and Kresge grants

Enlargement of special collections—trustee gift

New equipment and furniture for technical services—library funds, Pew Charitable Trust, and other grants

New conference room—Personal donation.

In addition, capital funds and a small amount from the library's operating budget were used where necessary to meet overruns on costs caused by problems within the building.

Project Analysis

Any large project will have problems. In this case, they were less financial than procedural. Keeping tabs on all expenditures proved to be a major task since at least four different budgets were involved and records from at least five university units (the library itself, the College of Arts and Sciences [for capital projects], development, computer services, buildings and grounds) had to be reconciled.

In order to satisfy the reporting requirements of the Kresge Foundation, the whole budget had to be recast to include the sprinkler project, and each phase had to be reported on separately, since the foundation would not release funds before the completion of each stage. In addition, the development office had to provide statements showing the exact nature of matching grants.

Other donors did not require the same detail, but reports had to be prepared showing the fulfillment of their aims. Some tail-end expenditures of Pew Charitable Trust funds for automation had to be cleared. Nearly all donors also had time limits for expenditure of their funds: Kresge, four years; Pew, five years; Surdna, three years. These overlapping time periods caused a severe strain on the accounting system, since none of them corresponded to the fiscal year of the university. At times, it became almost impossible to separate funding sources. Roof repair, for example, exceeded the amount set aside, even though the scope of the work had been reduced, and Kresge funds were used to make up the difference, with the foundation's approval. In the case of special collections, it was finally decided to allocate the entire cost to a trustee gift, rather than attempt to separate out individual components. This allowed the university to cover the added cost of replacing electrical wiring from other sources.

Donors and Their Needs

Multiple donors create not only recordkeeping problems; they also cause added anxiety until the gifts or grants are assured. The university followed the usual development adage that any major project requires a single major donor, in this case the Kresge Foundation, which carried the need for matching funds. Fortunately, these funds had already been solicited by the development office as part of starting up the new capital campaign. Other donations were seen by development as first installments on long-term possibilities, particularly since the expanded library figured largely in the new campaign. If that had not been the case, it might have been much more difficult to attract donors and necessary either to scale down the project or delay it while additional funding was sought. In any case, close cooperation with development was a key component.

The time taken to raise funds, report to donors, and provide adequate recognition was substantial, but helped maintain the library's track record in successful fundraising. One key element in the fundraising process was flexibility, for example, taking advice from the contractor and changing sequences when it was advantageous. All in all, the experience proved that it was possible to overhaul and modernize a building even while the building was in continuous use. The experience also proved that it was possible to attract donors for a whole series of library needs. The renovations had been preceded by a large automation grant from the Pew Charitable Trust, and by an even larger National Endowment for the Humanities (NEH) challenge grant, and it might have been thought that the library already had its "share." A clear statement of need, persistence by the library staff, ready support from the administration, and a good existing fundraising record overcame resistance from finance and development officers.

Conclusion

Despite the difficulties described here, the success of this project proved that it was possible for the library to attract funds. The fact that the library was able to function during four years of construction converted many who had previously been skeptical into believers, which provided a support base for further endeavors. The improved library pleased administrators, users, and staff. Whereas it would clearly have been preferable to handle a simpler project, it was possible, with persistence, to meld together several disparate activities. Keeping up staff morale required constant attention, and it was gratifying to find that the circulation staff could see the ultimate benefits clearly enough to put up with all the disruption and the added task of recovering needed materials from the closed stacks.

The result was a much more functional library, and, importantly, almost none of the renovations would have to be dismantled for the library expansion project. Since these conditions had been imposed by the administration, fulfilling them was important, not only to the success of the project, but also to further fundraising.

What lessons can be learned?

1. Keep It Simple. If this project were repeated, every effort would be made to keep it simpler, perhaps by separating the various subprojects. The difficulty with this was that all of the subprojects were interlinked: each stage depended on the completion of the ones before it. The university's insistence that the library remain open at all times tested everyone's ingenuity and also slowed down the project, since work virtually ceased during academic terms. Small exceptions could be made for special collections and the LAN installation, but that also meant revising the timetable.

2. Be Prepared for Problems. The major difficulty in this project arose from the sprinkler installation, because it involved stripping the ceiling from other parts of the library. Stack service was maintained for users by volunteer staff. Fortunately, there was no asbestos problem and dust levels were lower than expected.

Nevertheless, looking for books under plastic wraps laid over the stacks became burdensome. A proposal to close the library over the summer was rejected by the university administration. Instead, the library was allowed to close over a two-week term break, while major collections were rearranged. Staff and work crew enthusiasm helped to complete this project in less than two weeks.

3. *Do Your Homework.* Know what is involved. Map out a thorough plan before approaching anyone outside the library. Develop cost estimates and timetables to ensure that the proposal is realistic. In this case, the proposal needed several revisions, but because the original proposal was soundly conceived, the officials concerned were willing to be accommodating.

4. *Be Flexible.* Be flexible and willing to make changes in the project plan. Take the advice of those with experience, even if this means scaling back or altering some aspects of the project. In this project, the contractors were very helpful. Working closely with staff and work crews pays dividends.

5. *Have a Well-Developed Financial Plan.* Develop a clear financial strategy, working closely with the development office and the financial officers. Be aware and be sure that others are aware of any fund restrictions or time limits. The rule that there should be one major donor is important, whether the funds in question are from external sources—such as a foundation, an alumnus, or capital reserves—or a state appropriation. It is much easier to attract additional gifts and grants than to patch together a series of smaller gifts. If the principal costs are met from one major donor, thereby covering routine needs, it is possible to offer named rooms or areas in return for supplementary gifts. In this instance, no one would be likely to want a roof or a sprinkler system to be their memorial, but special rooms or collections are appropriate.

6. *Keep Control.* Keep on top of the project, and be sure that expenditures are properly allocated and good records are kept. Nothing is worse than having to explain fund cost overruns, or undoing inappropriate application of funds. Keeping the financial records clear may be difficult when several agencies are involved, but is essential for credibility.

7. *Cooperate.* Work hard with everyone to ensure that they are committed to the project—library staff, other university staff, contractors, and library users.

8. Recognize Contributions. Ensure that adequate thanks and recognition are given to donors. Even if donors have already received written letters or have been entertained by another department, do so again on behalf of the library. Recognize the help from staff, contractors, and other participants, both in writing and in a more tangible form, such as hosting a party.

Would the Wessell Library repeat the process described here? Every fundraising project has to stand on its own. In this case, there was no other way to proceed, and the same may be true of almost any building project. Much depends on the urgency of the need. If some work cannot be postponed and the scope exceeds the budget, then fundraising is a necessity. Try, however, to keep it as simple as possible. The more complex the project, the harder it is to explain and sell it. The fact that the university is now in the process of seeking funds for the expansion of the library indicates that the first project was seen as successful. Much will depend on the attitude of the principal donor. Donors such as the Kresge Foundation have a lot of experience and can be helpful in planning. Be prepared, however, for local resistance, since such a project can often be seen as competing with other goals. If there is no alternative, persistence is the key to success.

3 A Capital Campaign for a Small Public Library

Chanute, Kansas

JAMES SWAN

I first met Susan Willis, director of the Chanute, Kansas, Public Library, in the fall of 1989 at a meeting of the Kansas State Library Advisory Commission and the Library Services and Construction Act (LSCA) Council. The occasion was the awarding of Title II construction grants. Ms. Willis was there to observe the grant process because Chanute was planning a building project of its own.

That was about all I knew when I went to Chanute for a fundraising workshop in January of 1990. When I returned for the final dedication of the library and a museum in August of 1993, I saw a magnificently restored Santa Fe Railroad depot. Mike Mitchell, chair of the fundraising committee said, "We weren't going to accept that we couldn't get it done. We sold people on the idea that giving to the library project was an investment in the future of Chanute." A friend of the library said, "The whole town has really rallied behind the project." And so it seemed, but it took a lot of work to make it happen.

What started out as a straightforward plan to expand the library ended up being part of a multiphase downtown redevelopment project, the brainchild of a forward-thinking city manager, Robert Walker. His vision turned a ninety-year-old railroad depot into a library and a museum, which became the hub of a citywide redevelopment project. This is the story of how it all came together.

James Swan is the director of the Central Kansas Library System.

Old Train Depot Becomes a Library

The depot restoration committee was appointed following the city's purchase of the building in 1987 for $48,000. The committee was charged to:

Provide maintenance of the exterior of the depot to prevent further deterioration

Encourage people in the area to contribute to the project in its formative stages

Suggest plans for restoration and development of the grounds around the depot if the community expressed sufficient interest in the project.

Central to the discussion was the thought that uses of the depot should include the display of historical items, particularly items related to the period of the depot's construction in 1902 and the following years of service. Other suggested uses included meeting rooms, offices, shops, establishment of a branch public library for easier access to the disabled, and restoration of the Harvey House restaurant.

In April 1990, city manager Bob Walker announced a four-phase project that included renovation of the depot to house the Chanute Public Library and the Safari Museum. Mr. Walker said he developed the concept because of the need for space by both the museum and the library. "They complement each other so nicely," Mr. Walker said, "that that was the very birth of the idea. And we have been trying to find a good use for the depot since we bought it."

Both the library and museum boards had wanted to expand their facilities for years. The library had already hired an architect and had preliminary plans for an addition. The depot did not meet the ideal needs of either the public library or the museum, but both the curator of the museum and the librarian agreed that this building provided the best solution for both organizations.

Other aspects of the multiphase project included renovating the old library into a more spacious area for the District Court and Judicial Center, and the remodeling of the Memorial Auditorium.

Maurice Breidenthal, architect for the project and expert on remodeling historic buildings, said, "I had driven through town and had taken a picture of the depot for our files. I didn't know what Mr. Walker had up his sleeve, but it is an ingenious plan and I'm glad to be a part of it."

Lenore Kensett, library board president said, "When this project was presented we overwhelmingly felt the need to support it. Working together on this project will unite the citizens toward a common goal." The library board had looked at the depot earlier, but had dismissed the idea of using it for a library because it was too large for the library's needs and appeared to be too costly for the library to handle on its own.

Essential to the success of the project was a lead gift of $500,000 by Larry Hudson from the Larry D. Hudson Family Foundation. The foundation also later made a challenge grant of $250,000, which gave added incentive to community fundraising.

The combined fundraising effort was unique because its multi-faceted approach broadened the constituent base and made soliciting for donations easier. Those who wanted to support the library could see their dollars going for a new library. Lawyers could buy into the project because of the new District Court and Judicial Center. Museum supporters could help their favorite institution by giving to the project. Downtown merchants could secure their own future by investing in the project. And some people gave because they just wanted to see the depot saved. It was truly a win-win situation for everyone.

Communication was the key to success. The library staff and the board worked together at communicating to the community and city government the needs of the library. An extensive educational process was necessary to inform everyone of the library's present and future needs, the importance of the library in the community, and the potential for the new and improved services.

The staff worked closely with the architects to design an interior that was functional for a library. The librarian's advice to others contemplating a similar plan is:

Educate your community as to what a library is and should be before beginning the project. Unless community members see that a library will directly improve their lives, they will not support it.

Hire a professional fundraising consultant. The first step in this process must be a feasibility study to determine if the community will support the project financially. Also, get the consultant's advice on how to proceed.

Getting Started with a Fundraising Workshop

As mentioned earlier, I first met Susan Willis at an LSCA Council meeting. Afterward I spoke to her and offered to meet with her board and discuss fundraising. I had just submitted the manuscript for my book, *Fundraising for the Small Public Library: A How-to-Do-It Manual for Librarians* (Swan 1990). The library board invited me to Chanute for a half-day workshop on fundraising in January of 1990. (This was a few months before the announcement of the depot project.) They videotaped my presentation for those who were unable to attend.

Fundraising Workshop

In the workshop I presented for the library leaders, I reviewed many of the ideas from my book concerning capital fund drives. These included constituent building, selecting the fundraising chair, the chart of giving, and the use of professional fundraisers. After the project was completed, Susan Willis said, "The most important single thing we did was to hire a professional fundraiser. He helped us raise much more money than we ever dreamed we could."

Principles of Fundraising

Whereas asking potential donors for funds may be the most important step in fundraising, it is not a simple task. If it were, we could simply go and ask everyone for donations and money would come pouring in, and we would not need books on the subject. Fundraisers have developed techniques that help us organize our efforts and refine our methods to help us raise more money with less effort, and help us be successful more of the time.

The following five points are essential to any successful fundraising effort.

1. Know How Much You Need and the Purpose of Your Project. If you do not know the total cost of your project or why you need the money, your commitment will be weak. You do not need to share your goal with the donor, but you need to have it clearly in mind.

2. Give Before You Ask. Everyone who asks others for money must give to their cause themselves. They must give enough to make a difference in the cause or in their own lives.

3. Ask for the Gift. If you don't ask, you won't get (at least most of the time). Some libraries have been known to receive large gifts from unknown or unexpected sources. Don't count on it!

4. Ask the Right Person for the Right Amount. You don't pick one-pound tomatoes from a cherry tomato plant. You have to do your research if you want to know whom to ask for a big gift. Sometimes a professional fundraiser can help you identify the right person.

5. Say Thank You. Say "thank you" in as many ways as you can. And recognize everyone who helped. Someone has said that you have to say thank you seven times before you can ask for another gift.

The people who led the Chanute project did a good job of following these five points. They had a tangible goal of $2 million to renovate the Santa Fe depot.

The second point was critical to the success of the Chanute project. If you do not give before you ask, you will not be convincing. Psychologists have discovered that people who ask others for donations without giving themselves are less effective than those who have given. People who have given can say, "I gave to the project; now it is your turn." People who have given are confident and committed.

Asking for the gift is best done in person, face to face, by someone who has given a similar amount. In Chanute a lot of people did a lot of asking, and they were all committed to the project. Donors are usually qualified by the amount of money they have to give and their interest in giving to your project. The Chanute project brought together several diverse constituents and capitalized on their willingness to give to any one aspect of the project.

Saying thank you is critical to the success of every fundraising effort. Besides the notes of gratitude and praise, the people in Chanute had a gala preview.

On March 24, 1992, about two hundred contributors came to see what their money had purchased. Dressed for a gala opening night celebration, they were overwhelmed to see the transformation of the old depot. City manager Robert Walker said, "This was in part a wish of the steering committee to involve those who had been actively involved in the project—so they could see the results of their efforts."

Chart of Giving

Professional fundraiser Robert Hartsook recommends developing a chart of giving similar to Figure 3.1. This represents the high end of the giving scale. He believes that the goal is possible if the fundraising group can confidently write down three names for each gift sought. Some donors will not give at the anticipated level, but may give at a lower level. This chart should be seen as a target, not as a hard and fast rule. No capital campaign ever matches the chart of giving exactly, but they often average out closely. The chart targets eighteen donors to give 40 percent of the money.

		Campaign Goal: $1,000,000		
	Number	*Amount*	*Percent*	*Names*
Lead gift	1	$100,000	10	_____
				_____
				_____
Lead gifts	2	$ 50,000	10	_____
				_____
				_____
				_____
Major gifts	5	$ 25,000	10	_____
				_____
				_____
				_____
Big gifts	10	$ 10,000	10	_____
				_____
				_____
				_____

Figure 3.1   Chart of Giving

The chart of giving sets the goal for the capital campaign. In sporting activities, goals are prominent—teams win by crossing home plate, crossing the goal line with the football, or throwing the basketball through the hoop. Goals let everyone know where the team is headed. Writing the goal down is critical to success. Many successful fundraising projects display a thermometer-like goal to chart the success of their campaign.

The Chanute project was successful primarily because the lead gift was 37.5 percent of the goal. In all, nineteen contributors donated over 68 percent of the money.

Professional Fundraisers

In the workshop I suggested hiring a professional fundraiser.

> Raising major dollar support is much like restoring an irreplaceable book . . . it involves meticulous planning and perseverance. The process of formulating needs, building an effective appeal, and raising major funding requires leadership exhibiting three traits:
>
> *Desire to learn*—taking in; soaking up; becoming full of knowledge pertaining to your institution; where you've been, where you're going, and how you're going to get there
>
> *Provide challenge and vision*—leading; inspiring others to seek and achieve
>
> *Discipline*—planning; executing; persevering through completion of the goal. (Vance Associates)

A professional fundraiser is trained to do all of the above. Libraries that want to raise $250,000 or more need to hire a fundraiser. Well-meaning amateurs can raise perhaps a third of what they need, but it takes the expertise of the professional to get all the money the library needs.

You can expect a professional to do the following:

Conduct a feasibility or precampaign study

Review and refine your library's mission statement

Interview community leaders

Help select a campaign leader

Assist in setting a realistic goal for the project

Help write and prepare a case statement

Formulate gift brackets to reach the goal

Train leaders to recruit volunteers

Train volunteer solicitors

Help get the campaign started

Keep the campaign moving

Manage the campaign office

Formulate the total campaign calendar

Provide guidance for large-gift cultivation

Write special proposals

Prepare public relations materials

Develop follow-up procedures.

For the skeptics in the workshop I suggested completing the quiz shown in Figure 3.2.

You may not need a professional fundraiser if you answered "yes" to all of the questions in Figure 3.2. The first question is critical—raising less than $250,000 can probably be on your own. That is not to say that you would not benefit from the assistance of a professional. Kenneth M. Vance of Fundraising Consultants from LeMars, Iowa, feels that the return on the investment below this amount may be questionable.

Conducting a Feasibility or Precampaign Study

A reputable fundraiser will want to do a feasibility study before embarking on a full-blown campaign. If the money is not there, it is better to find that out before launching a campaign.

Vance Associates say that the pre-campaign study is the prelude to the actual campaign. It forms the foundation and direction for all planning. It should answer the following questions:

How much money can be raised?

Where are the funds coming from?

Who will be the most effective chairperson?

What is the best timetable?

	Yes	No
Do we want to raise less than $250,000?	____	____
Do we have a clear vision of what we want to do and how we want to do it?	____	____
Do members of our organization have the skills to assess the giving potential for our project in our community?	____	____
Do we know who will lead us and are we confident that he or she can manage the campaign?	____	____
Can we train our volunteers to be highly effective solicitors?	____	____
Can we count on every member of the board to be committed to the project and give a sacrificial gift?	____	____
Can we recruit people to help us sell our vision to others in a way that will raise money?	____	____
Do we have the skills and resources within our organization to develop quality written materials to support our project?	____	____
Can we write and produce a persuasive, polished case statement?	____	____

Figure 3.2   Professional Fundraiser Readiness Quiz

Most of all, it begins the process of building ownership in the campaign.

The time required for an effective precampaign study will vary depending on the geographical location of the institution's constituency and the number of interviews conducted. Professional fundraisers begin the process by compiling a short list of community leaders. The list is generated from a meeting of community leaders who have an interest in the organization. As consultants interview members of this group, they ask them for the names of other community leaders. The consultants get a sense of the community and its attitudes about the organization. They also gain an awareness of where the deep pockets are and if there is an interest in the library.

During this interview process, the professional fundraisers are looking for which person would be perceived by the community to be the best leader of the fundraising campaign. This is one of the major advantages of using a professional fundraiser. The library board may have handpicked someone for the task of leading the fundraising campaign, yet the community may not perceive that person to be the most effective one for the job. An outsider helping to select the leader for the campaign can add credibility to the effort and can help overcome any cronyism.

One professional fundraiser likes to interview at least thirty persons for each campaign. First, this fundraiser asks the individuals how they feel about the library. Is it meeting their needs? Could it do a better job? If so, how? He has two documents with him—a list of library needs and their estimated costs, and a scale of giving. After reviewing the list of needs with the person he is interviewing, he explains that in order for the library to meet its needs, it has to raise a certain amount of money. Then he shows the interviewee the chart of giving and asks how many gifts of a certain size the interviewee thinks can be raised in the community. Sometimes without being asked, the interviewee volunteers to make the lead gift.

In the Chanute project, Robert Hartsook was hired to conduct the feasibility study. Mr. Hartsook made a special trip to Chanute to accompany the city manager, Robert Walker, on a visit to Larry Hudson regarding the lead gift. Later on, one of Mr. Hartsook's associates, Beth Fager, helped organize the campaign. She met with the board to map out strategies and develop approaches; she also trained volunteers with role-playing techniques, and kept the group focused.

After Ms. Fager's initial work was done, the committee took charge of its own destiny. Mike Mitchell, chair of the committee, said, "We took control of the project ourselves. We just sold the project as an investment in the future of Chanute."

It is possible to do your own feasibility study. But do not be too quick to jump into the task. The information gathered from visits with community leaders will not be as accurate if you do it yourself. They will tell you what they think you want to hear, and not always what they think is the truth.

Selecting the Chair

In the workshop, we also talked about selecting the fundraising committee. Part of the professional's job in the preliminary study is to help select the chair of the capital campaign committee. The chair should be someone who is capable of making a major gift and has an interest in the cause. Otherwise, other large gifts will not come in.

You need to interview everyone you are considering for committee chair. Write a job description for the position. Take this document with you when you visit the people you have selected as possible candidates for the job. Do not initially tell them they are chair candidates. Ask each one what they think of the draft document. Ask them if they can think of anything you left out or should have included. You can also show them a draft copy of the case statement and the chart of giving. Their reactions to your questions will be revealing. The people you visit will begin to internalize the purpose of your visit—that is, they will begin to see themselves in the role of committee chair, without your asking them. They will begin to think of their own contribution to the fund drive. Below is a sample job description for the committee chair position.

Fundraising Committee Chair

(Job Description)

The Chair of the Capital Fund Drive Committee will be expected to:

Be absolutely committed to the project

Make a significant gift

Ask for the lead gift—the single largest gift—or help someone else do it

Recruit five team leaders

Be enthusiastic about raising money for the library

Generate that same enthusiasm in others

Know everything about the library's fundraising project

Be friendly to everyone in town

Use personal influence for the good of the library

Know the committee system and delegate effectively

Work with the people who may express differing opinions

Never doubt victory.

In Chanute, Robert Hartsook helped identify possible committee chairs, but he did not make the final selection. The people who made the selection had all of the above points in mind as they made their selection.

The person they selected made the second highest gift. Professional fundraisers have found that other major gifts tend to cluster around the largest gift made by key members of the committee. Robert Hartsook told the library board they had to find someone who could make a substantial contribution to be the chair of the fundraising campaign. If a group wants to raise $1,000,000, therefore, the right to be chair of the fundraising committee may involve a $50,000 or $100,000 contribution.

With the project well underway in the fall of 1991, the library board applied for an LSCA Title II construction grant and received $100,000.

On January 16, 1992, the depot project reached its fundraising goal of $2,000,000 with a last minute gift of $30,000. Eighty percent of the total came from nineteen contributors. The largest amount, $750,000 (37.5 percent of the total), came from the Larry D. Hudson Family Foundation. Eighteen gifts exceeded $25,000. More than 330 other pledges and donations came from individuals, families, and businesses.

Conclusion

The Chanute depot restoration project was successful for several reasons:

1. Robert Walker, the city manager, had a clear vision of the entire project. He was able to communicate his vision and enlisted the support of others.
2. Larry Hudson and the Larry Hudson Family Foundation made the fundraising effort possible.

3. The library board had the courage to hire Robert Hartsook, a professional fundraiser. He help them raise much more money than they could have done on their own.
4. The project had broad-based constituent support. Those who wanted to support a particular part of the project could support the whole project and know that their favorite segment would be helped.

Notes

Swan, James. 1990. *Fundraising for the small public library.* New York: Neal-Schuman.

Vance Associates, fundraising consultants, Le Mars, Iowa. Personal communication.

CHAPTER 4

Establishing a Library Foundation and a Fundraising Campaign

JENNYE E. GUY

The year 1985 was a pivotal one for the Atlanta-Fulton public library system. The residents of the city of Atlanta and Fulton County, having transferred the library system from the city to the county and having tired of using a library system that showed the effects of years of neglect and underfunding, passed a $38 million bond referendum mandating significant changes and major capital improvements for the public library system. The voters wanted a library system that did more than provide the basics in services and resources. They wanted their system to be an enduring resource, rich with in-depth materials covering a broad spectrum of information needs.

By 1987, planning for the bond referendum projects was completed and initial implementation was under way. At that time, the library system's Board of Trustees approved the concept of expanding the Samuel Williams Collection on the Black Experience and building a special facility to house it. This expansion ultimately resulted in the collection becoming the Auburn Avenue Research Library on African-American Culture and History.

The $38 million bond referendum, coupled with a sizeable increase in the library system's county-funded budget over a two-year period, had empowered the library system to make long over-

---

Jennye E. Guy is the development officer for the Atlanta-Fulton public library system.

due service and resource improvements. But those resources were insufficient to revitalize the library system and create excellence as well. Uniform excellence therefore became the library system's goal—how to achieve it was the question.

One of the methods the library system adopted in its quest for excellence was to create a private, nonprofit foundation whose sole function would be to seek, receive, and administer private gifts on behalf of the library system. Of the many areas in which private funds could be used to strengthen and enhance resources, the transformation of the Samuel Williams Collection on the Black Experience into a special research library became, over time, the most critical.

Using the project of securing funding for collection of the Auburn Avenue Research Library on African-American Culture and History, this case study illustrates: (1) how the library system and the library foundation conducted their first major private fundraising campaign; (2) the problems, situations, and opportunities that arose during the campaign, and (3) the lessons the campaign taught.

The Starting Point

Until the library can demonstrate that funds are well managed and well spent and that they still are not enough, a campaign will not be successful.
—Feasibility study interviewee

Within many public facilities there is a special place for private support.
—Feasibility study interviewee

From its thirty-two facilities, including the downtown central library, the Atlanta-Fulton public library system serves the nearly seven hundred thousand residents of the city of Atlanta and Fulton County. These residents present a wide spectrum of informational, recreational, and educational needs: from scholars doing independent research to preschoolers wanting stories read to them, from entrepreneurs analyzing business opportunities to new citizens acquiring English as a second language to help them create lives here. The library system attempts to meet all these demands with a staff of over five hundred persons and a budget of approximately $21 million.

Because it is one of fifty-one departments under the auspices of Fulton County, the Atlanta-Fulton public library system must share the county's budget resources. Even though the library system's administration and Board of Trustees determine its priorities and the resulting budget request, the actual budget level is set and funded by the Fulton County Board of Commissioners.

Despite a two-year funding increase, the library system's budget had become static. Meanwhile, the public's demands upon the system's resources and calls for increases in library service and materials were growing. Increased library use, coupled with the stationary funding base, caused the library system to consider funding alternatives to upgrade targeted areas. The Board of Trustees wrestled with the dilemma of how to obtain additional funding for those areas in which the system needed to improve and expand—chiefly the proposed Auburn Avenue Research Library on African-American Culture and History.

The Board of Trustees was definite about maintaining its role solely as the library system's policy-setting body. Another group would therefore have to guide the library system through any fundraising efforts. Thus, the idea of creating a library foundation with its own governing body was born. Three persons (two trustees and the library director) formed the library foundation's initial Board of Directors. Under their leadership, the library foundation applied for and received 501(c)(3) status. The original, and all future library foundation directors, were officially charged with seeking and receiving gifts on behalf of the library system.

Now the library system had the main qualification necessary for approaching potential donors—accountability. By giving the library system an identity apart from its government affiliation, the library foundation could assure donors that gifts would not be usurped by government or used in ways other than what was intended.

Empowered by the trustees to find and use private funds to help create the library system's margin of excellence, the library foundation decided to make its first fundraising effort a $4.6 million campaign to seek gifts for: the library system's literacy program, several special collections, interior completion of the third and fourth floors of the Auburn Avenue Research Library's building, and the Research Library's opening day collection.

Of those targeted areas, seeking funds for both the building and collection of the Auburn Avenue Research Library on African-American Culture and History was the most challenging. With a special facility being constructed on historic Auburn Avenue in

Atlanta, the Research Library was using the central library's Samuel Williams Collection on the Black Experience as the core around which to develop the rest of its collection. Even though it was designed to be a research library whose holdings would not circulate, access to the collections would not be restricted. This approach would give the public access to information and collections normally reserved for scholars in private institutions and homes. The Research Library would also preserve and conserve historic books and publications, audiovisual items, documents, archival materials, and art. The building would provide the community with facilities for meetings, seminars, teleconferences, and private study. In addition, the Research Library would host programs, events, and seminars related to its materials and subjects, as well as exhibit items from the library system's collections, and from other sources.

The time and location were right to build this unique facility. A distinctive aspect of Atlanta's culture is its large African-American population. In Fulton County, an area that includes most of Atlanta, over half of the residents are African-American. The city houses the Atlanta University Center, a unique consortium of seven historically black colleges and universities, including a medical school. Many of yesterday's and today's African-American leaders have lived and worked in Atlanta. Martin Luther King Jr. led the civil rights movement from Atlanta, placing the city in the center of this historic period. In 1973, Maynard Jackson (a former member of the library system's Board of Trustees) became Atlanta's first black mayor, ushering in an era of political power for African-Americans that has produced leaders such as former Mayor Andrew Young.

As for Auburn Avenue itself, it boasted several historic "firsts": the first black daily newspaper chain, the first banks founded and run by blacks in Georgia, and the first two insurance companies started and managed by blacks in Georgia.

From the early 1900s to the 1950s, Auburn Avenue was a thriving black commercial, residential, social, and religious district. Many noted entertainers such as Black Patti, Cab Calloway, and Dinah Washington performed regularly at the famous Royal Peacock Lounge and the Top Hat Club. The state's first black professional building was on Auburn Avenue. In 1912, the Oddfellows Building and later the Oddfellows Auditorium were erected at a total cost of $430,000, typifying the business and financial acumen that flourished in the Auburn Avenue district. The street also contained many of the finest examples of Victorian architecture in the city, for the area was home to Atlanta's black elite. Three churches, which later became synonymous with significant social movements, are Auburn Avenue landmarks: Wheat Street Baptist and Ebenezer Baptist Churches, and Big Bethel African Methodist Episcopal Church. Auburn Avenue figured prominently in the civil rights movement by providing the headquarters for the Southern Christian Leadership Conference and Martin Luther King Jr.'s efforts. Notably, Martin Luther King Jr. was born on Auburn Avenue.

Grants from the state of Georgia and Fulton County had allowed the library system to design and begin constructing the Research Library's four-story, 50,000-square-foot building. It would be the capstone of the library system's capital improvements program.

Getting Ready

Where is the downtown library?
— Feasibility study interviewee

A local fundraising firm was hired to guide the library foundation through the campaign. The firm's first step in preparing for the campaign was to conduct a feasibility study to determine the community's willingness to support a fundraising campaign on behalf of the library system.

In-depth interviews with thirty business, civic, and philanthropic leaders were conducted during an eighteen-week period beginning in December of 1987 and ending in mid-April of 1988. The responses were mixed—ranging from staunch support of the library system and the community's need for its services to ignorance of the central library's location.

The feasibility study confirmed for the library system many of the weaknesses it had already identified. The study found that the library system:

Had a low profile image among the public—despite lobbying in 1985 for a bond referendum

Had a reputation for poor service

Housed inadequate collections

Was perceived as being governmental, thereby foregoing the need for private support.

Surprisingly, despite these findings, the study's overall conclusion was that the community would support a library foundation campaign.

All of these problems had to be addressed before fundraising could begin, however. The feasibility study recommended steps the library system could take to improve its image and reputation in the community. A detailed timeline was developed outlining these actions, both before and during the fundraising campaign. Key among those steps was a public awareness program aimed at raising the public's perception of the library system as a valued community resource.

In order to improve the community's perception of the library system, extensive systemwide improvements needed to be made. A $38 million bond referendum passed in 1985 by Fulton County voters had already given the library system the opportunity to make those changes. The bond referendum enabled the library system to:

Construct thirteen new buildings

Install three rail transit kiosk libraries

Expand one facility

Renovate the central library and complete two unfinished floors.

Construct and install six mini-libraries

Improve and upgrade the library system's general collections and start collections at the newly built branches

Buy a new computer system.

By the time the feasibility study was finished, the most visible of the bond referendum's mandates had been started—improving and expanding the library system's physical plant. The construction program was ambitious. Beginning in 1988 and continuing over the next twenty-four months, the library system would break ground for nearly twenty new or renovated facilities. Within the following thirty-six months, those buildings would open. While the construction program was under way, the library system upgraded the old computer; made plans to design and install a new computer network and other electronic information services; bought more than five hundred thousand books for the branches' collections; and implemented an intensive customer service training program.

The construction projects created natural occasions for ongoing image building. Thus, the decision was made to use the bond referendum-mandated improvements as the platform for the public awareness program. This was done by making every groundbreaking (and later, the new branches' opening celebrations) the focus of intensive media exposure. The groundbreakings afforded ideal press opportunities that highlighted the following concepts.

> Each library branch was designed to complement its surrounding community. A range of styles by different architects was featured, with one branch winning a national architectural design award.

> Neighborhoods throughout the seventy-mile length of Fulton County received new buildings. Community and metropolitan newspapers covered the groundbreakings.

> The theme of "responsive excellence" was promoted with each new service improvement or technological innovation. Each library branch would be a part of the improved computer and electronic network. The new buildings and expanded collections offered proof that the library system was serious about giving excellent service to the neighborhoods it served.

The strategy worked. Slowly, the library system began to create a reputation for being responsive to the communities it served, innovative in its programs and resources, and progressive in its planning to meet patrons' needs. These perceptions would be helpful when the library foundation courted business and private funding sources.

The feasibility study had a second purpose: to determine how large a campaign the private sector would support. Interviewees were asked about the size of gifts they would consider making. The feasibility study showed that a $4.6 million campaign was possible; whether the library foundation could actually reach that goal remained to be seen.

On the Campaign Trail

The campaign will need an honorary chair from the public sector —preferably the governor.

—Feasibility study interviewee

*Leadership is the key to any campaign's success. Nothing
else matters.*
                              —Feasibility study interviewee

As the library system improved services and constructed buildings,
the library foundation began cultivating its membership. Early in
the campaign the decision was made to have the library foundation's directors serve as its leadership and volunteers, with additional directors being carefully sought and added to the Board as the
campaign progressed. Several considerations led to this decision.

> It would be more effective in the long run to build a body of
> dedicated library system volunteers whose main responsi-
> bility was to oversee fundraising efforts rather than recruit
> temporary spokespersons on a project-by-project basis.

> Who else could tell the library system's story as convincingly as
> those who were most knowledgeable of and committed to
> its success?

> Since the library system was having to create a foundation any-
> way, why not recruit as directors some of the people whom
> it would eventually ask to support the campaign?

At the start, the campaign's chief players were the library foundation's first three directors: its chair, a community leader with
strong ties to the local philanthropic community and who was also
the chair of the Board of Trustees; a state senator who was a partner
in a leading law firm and a former chair of the Board of Trustees;
and the library director. The president of the fundraising firm was
the fourth campaign leader. Staff support was provided by the
library system's development office.

Encouraged by the library system's success at improving its
image and standing in the community, the library foundation decided to target its first fundraising attempts toward the National
Endowment for the Humanities (NEH) and a major local foundation. It was felt that gifts from these particular donors would give a
"Good Housekeeping Seal of Approval" to the campaign, thereby
making it easier to solicit more gifts and reach the $4.6 million goal.

The two requests were submitted simultaneously. The foundations were asked for gifts to any of the areas they wished to consider. Both were denied. The library foundation would have to wait
one year before it could resubmit proposals to the organizations.

Several valuable lessons were learned from the rejection of these grant proposals. The first was to narrow the fundraising focus. A decision was made to divide the campaign into two phases conducted over several years. Whereas funding for the same areas would still be sought, the amounts would be scaled down in the first phase. Entitled "Open a New Chapter: Be a Partner with the Library," the campaign's phase one was now a $2.7 million drive to obtain gifts to be used to improve the business, southern literature and history, and genealogy collections; expand the literacy program; finish the third and fourth floors of the Auburn Avenue Research Library's building; and develop the Auburn Library's collection in time for its opening day.

Another lesson learned from this experience was to identify and cultivate donors before asking them to give. The library foundation decided to refrain from making requests and use the yearlong waiting period to intensively cultivate donors. The foundation also decided to approach the NEH and the major local foundation again at a later time since their support was still deemed critical to the campaign's overall success.

The major local foundation had been visited by library foundation directors once before the first ill-fated proposal was submitted. Apparently, that level of cultivation had not been sufficient. During the yearlong waiting period that followed, the major local foundation visited the central library several times and became intimately acquainted with the library system. The president of the major local foundation and the library director also met periodically to review the library system's progress with service improvements and the construction program. By the time the second proposal was submitted, the major local foundation knew both the library system and the library foundation well and had confidence in their leadership.

While a solid relationship with the major local foundation was being established, the library foundation decided to host a series of presentations to cultivate potential donors and introduce business and philanthropic leaders to the library system. The library foundation's chair and the library director led educational forums on the services and resources of the library system. Only one guest at a time was invited to the central library; this guest could bring one or two colleagues if desired. During these sessions, an in-depth presentation on the library system—featuring displays of collection highlights, handouts, and explanations of current services and resources, plans, and improvements—was made by the library director. After his remarks, the library foundation's chair talked about the need for a library foundation and the goal of supporting library system initiatives, especially those of the campaign.

In addition to serving as an opportunity to make friends for the library system, these public relations presentations were used to explore the guests' funding interests. In many cases, guests would frankly state the areas they preferred to fund and suggest amounts to request. Their remarks were helpful when the library foundation returned to make formal requests of their respective organizations.

A variation of the public relations presentations was the corporate breakfast, designed to introduce groups of influential people to the library system. Three breakfasts were held, and approximately twenty leaders from media, business, and education attended each one. Again, at each breakfast the library foundation chair and library director made a presentation about the library system, highlighting services and improvements. Whereas no direct appeals were made during the breakfasts, guests understood that the library foundation would follow up their visit with a request.

Both the small group meetings and the corporate breakfasts were effective in cultivating potential donors and making friends for the library system and its foundation. For example, when the library system faced budget cuts by Fulton County, the goodwill created by these forums caused the public to speak up on its behalf. The result was that the severity of the proposed budget cuts was lessened.

After spending approximately one-and-one-half years on intense donor cultivation, the library foundation resumed the campaign. Analysis of the feedback received from the potential donor presentations and the corporate breakfasts showed that the campaign needed to be refined once more and its focus narrowed even further. Of the phase one goals, which should remain and which should be deferred for future fundraising efforts? The library foundation's deliberations were partially affected by the fact that by this time, additional funding to complete the Auburn Avenue Research Library's building had been secured through Fulton County. Thus, funding was needed to develop the Research Library's collection in time for its planned opening in 1993.

After a third restructuring, the campaign's new focus was to acquire funding for the Auburn Avenue Research Library's opening day collection. Whereas gifts to the other phase one goals would be welcomed, they would not be actively sought.

Returning to the major local foundation, the library foundation requested a $500,000 lead gift. The major local foundation was also informed that the NEH would be asked for a $500,000 challenge grant to help develop the Auburn Avenue Research Library's opening day collection. A lead gift from the major local foundation would serve two strategic purposes: (1) it would bolster the library foundation's request to NEH, and (2) it would help leverage other gifts to meet the three-to-one match required by NEH if the library foundation's proposal was approved.

Success came quickly the second time around as the new, streamlined proposals to the major local foundation and NEH were approved. The major local foundation timed its $500,000 gift so that the library foundation could report to NEH that a significant gift had already been given to the Auburn Avenue Research Library's opening day collection. As hoped, this gift greatly strengthened the application to NEH and is believed to be largely responsible for the resulting $400,000 grant to the library foundation.

Armed with these two pivotal gifts of $500,000 from the major local foundation and a $400,000 challenge grant from the NEH, the library foundation launched its redesigned fundraising effort: a $1.2 million campaign to match the challenge grant from the NEH to develop the Auburn Avenue Research Library's opening day collection.

The campaign was a well-thought out process and therefore was destined for success. In addition to raising $1.2 million for the Auburn Avenue Research Library, the library foundation's efforts resulted in other significant gifts that have greatly enhanced the library system's services to the public. Some of the gifts the library foundation obtained while the campaign was under way include over $30,000 for literacy, $158,000 for a pilot project to deliver electronic library service to a special-needs community, and $15,000 for a special collection on the Japanese language and culture.

Looking Back: Some Reflections

"Great" is the only goal worth having. Quality is more important than quantity. The library should seek greatness.
                                   —Feasibility study interviewee

People can't say no to the library. I like that it's fundamental. With my money I will be able to encourage and endorse a project that is already doing well.
                                   —Feasibility study interviewee

The library foundation's pursuit of greatness for the library system during this first fundraising campaign encountered unexpected situations that made flexibility and openness to change implicit requirements for ultimate success. For example, the campaign timeline prepared during the feasibility study stage quickly lost its usefulness, and was finally discarded in favor of deadlines imposed by the NEH grant. In order to receive annual grant installments from NEH, the library foundation had to certify that specified matching gift levels had been reached during the preceding year. The fundraising and reporting deadlines of the NEH therefore became the campaign's timetable.

The campaign suffered a major setback when a proposal that had been submitted to a national foundation was denied. Identified as an influential funder from whom a grant would help leverage other national and local gifts, the campaign was counting heavily on this foundation's support to help reach the $1.2 million goal. The whole process—from application to this foundation to refusal—lasted approximately eighteen months and involved a visit to the foundation, countless phone calls, and several submissions of periodically updated reports.

In addition to the problems encountered in raising money, establishing the library foundation's Board of Directors did not move as smoothly as planned. First, it took much longer than anyone had imagined to recruit and form a solid core of directors who would also serve as volunteers. Second, Board member turnover was high, making board development a constant concern in addition to that of raising money. Third, Board leadership changed just prior to the campaign's conclusion, affecting the campaign's momentum somewhat as time was spent in selecting another chair.

Encouraged by the success of this campaign, the library foundation is looking ahead to other projects to build on the excellent foundation of this campaign. Because of the intensive public relations aspect of this fundraising campaign, the public's awareness and appreciation of the library system have increased, and the public is now open to being a partner in the library system's vision and goals. The library fund can now count on the public to help it achieve its vision and goals for the library system.

This first campaign taught many invaluable lessons—lessons that should make mounting future campaigns easier. Of those lessons, the most important is: libraries have a fair chance for a piece of the philanthropic pie—their leaders have to be vigorous, tenacious, and creative in pursuing it.

5 The Challenge of the Challenge Grant

Johns Hopkins Library Endowment

KENNETH E. FLOWER

In December 1987, Johns Hopkins University was awarded a National Endowment for the Humanities (NEH) challenge grant of $1 million, which required the university to raise $4 million in qualifying new gifts. Hopkins was one of twenty-nine educational and cultural institutions in seventeen states receiving grants totaling $12.2 million from NEH that year. NEH awarded only four challenge grants of the maximum amount ($1 million) in 1987.

The NEH grant was to support improvement of the humanities collections of the Milton S. Eisenhower Library, the main library at the university. Despite the fact that Hopkins has been an international center for research and teaching since its founding in 1876, a central library was only created in 1964 when the Eisenhower Library was built at Homewood. Prior to that time, departmental libraries predominated with strong but narrowly focused collections. The humanities collections needed to be expanded, and the demands of new interdisciplinary programs needed to be addressed. The library had an inadequate base of endowment and was overly dependent upon current revenues. The challenge grant addressed these problems in part, and its fundraising period overlapped the

Kenneth E. Flower is associate director for administrative services at Milton S. Eisenhower Library, Johns Hopkins University. He acknowledges the valuable assistance of Ellen Stifler, director of development at the Eisenhower Library, in preparing this chapter.

broader Campaign for Johns Hopkins, which had started several years earlier with a university-wide goal of $450 million. When these campaigns ended, both goals had been exceeded. The over $5 million raised for the NEH challenge created a permanent endowment dedicated to the acquisition of crucial humanities materials.

A Long-Shot?

To some, the Eisenhower Library's NEH challenge grant looked like a long shot from the beginning. Whereas an informal assessment was made as to the potential fundraising capability of the library, a feasibility study was not done. Some even believed that, had a formal study been done, Hopkins may not have asked for such a large grant from NEH. And despite having one of the oldest Friends of the Libraries groups in the country, the library did not have a robust record in fundraising.

During the campaign, changes in key library and university officers created difficulties, and the normal four-year campaign was extended with NEH's permission to five years. This period saw a change in the university's president, a new provost, two library directors (as well as a one-year interim director), and several library development officers. Nevertheless, the university rose to the occasion and what one generation began, another completed.

Origin of the Campaign

The idea for the campaign was born from discussion between the library and the School of Arts and Sciences. It grew from a long-felt understanding of the inadequacy of the library's collections to support the world-class level of Hopkins research. The university was founded with a dependence on neighboring collections and developed for almost ninety years without the tradition of a strong central library.

When discussions began to find the right approach for the university's request to NEH for a second challenge grant (the university received its first NEH challenge grant in 1978), the development officer for the library was on the staff of the School of Arts and Sciences (both the library and Arts and Sciences report to the provost). Later reorganization moved the director of library development to report jointly to the library director and university central development. The initial organizational arrangement between the library and Arts and Sciences provided an important link that encouraged collaboration to begin. Staff of the School of Arts and Sciences and the library produced a proposal to NEH; NEH considered the proposal exceptional and later included it with sample proposals sent to other prospective applicants.

The Magic of a Challenge

A challenge gift or grant is a powerful fundraising strategy. Challenge grants, unlike strict matching gift arrangements, encourage giving to a set goal before challenge funds are released. The thought of possibly losing a challenge gift acts as an incentive to volunteers and is a marvelous selling point to prospects. The NEH challenge established not only a final goal, but goals for the end of each year within the campaign. NEH made these milestones critical by releasing federal funds each year only when certification occurred. One major donor relished being able to help direct federal dollars to a cause he fully supported. Each challenge year ended in the summer and, as a result, the timing for achieving challenge year annual goals did not conflict with the typical high giving level at the end of each calendar year for tax purposes. Two deadlines each year were therefore available for staff to encourage donors to give.

Daunting Fundraising Requirements

This particular grant was the second of its kind for Hopkins, so it required a match of four-to-one. NEH provided a twenty-five-page document detailing the administrative requirements of the challenge grant. Not only were the reporting requirements described, but specific criteria concerning matching requirements and gift eligibility were presented. NEH's basic requirements for all matching funds were: (1) that the gifts must be from new donors or be an increase over the amount given by a donor during the base year (the year prior to the beginning of the grant period); (2) gifts must be given in response to the challenge grant; (3) gifts must be used for approved purposes described in the application; and (4) gifts must be made during the challenge period.

The challenge grant period was initially four years and fundraising goals were set at the end of each year. Whereas these

detailed and specific requirements may have appeared overly burdensome at the outset—and indeed were time-consuming throughout—the benefits far outweighed the difficulties. The eligibility
guidelines inspired new donors and increased giving from existing
donors. Eligible gifts-in-kind, namely suitable humanities materials, could be counted toward the challenge, but were not widely
sought, with the exception of a few important personal collections
and individual works. Throughout the campaign and afterward,
library staff maintained their ongoing, thorough review of all potential gifts-in-kind, since these may often be more trouble than they
are worth.

Keys to Success

The success of the challenge grant can be attributed to a number of
factors, including committed donors and professional staff with the
full support of university officers. The effort was led very capably
by both library directors during this period, as well as the interim
director and respective library development officers. In addition to
the resources available from the Johns Hopkins development
office, the university's nationally based Library Advisory Council
and the Johns Hopkins Friends of the Libraries were instrumental.
The Friends group was particularly helpful in serving as a mecha-
nism for donor cultivation by identifying and involving individuals
particularly interested in libraries.

The response from the community was very positive—many
readily recognized the need. Although support was widespread, the
success of the campaign was possible primarily because of the commitment and generosity of a handful of wealthy donors. The
library's most generous donor gave almost $1.8 million to the NEH
challenge grant and over $600,000 on an additional $1.5 million
pledge to endow the position of library director. Filling in behind
the major donors were several thousand supportive contributors of
smaller gifts. In terms of the number and size of gifts received over
the five years of the campaign, there were 23 gifts of $100,000 or
more (3 above $500,000), 6 gifts from $50,000 to $100,000, 269 gifts
from $1,000 to $50,000, and 6,920 gifts received in amounts below
$1,000. There were 4,183 donors to the NEH challenge during this
period and another 2,358 non-NEH donors during the same period.
This count includes donors whose contributions were gifts-in-kind.

A surprising number of gifts were received from library and university staff. Faculty response to the challenge was quite supportive although a specifically designed Faculty Endowment for the Humanities did not elicit a large response. The library lacked a significant base of donors prior to the campaign, so the length of the challenge grant gave the library a valuable opportunity to cultivate potential donors. This was a significant factor in the campaign's success.

Meeting the NEH challenge was important to the university for a number of reasons. One was the importance of establishing a firm base for future campaigns by ensuring the success of the current campaign. This commitment to the success of the NEH campaign did occur, not only from both university presidents during this period, but also from key university vice-presidents. One university vice-president, in fact, was instrumental in introducing what would be the most significant donor to the library and to the NEH campaign. Whereas individual giving was the greatest source of contributions, a number of key corporate and foundation gifts (including a $500,000 gift) was also encouraged at the presidential level. Library development staff needed to engage key university officials actively to assist in identifying prospective donors. The campaign owes much of its success to the fullest support of university administrators at the highest levels.

A unique aspect to this particular campaign was a particularly appealing method of donor recognition. In its campaign to build endowment for library humanities materials, the challenge capitalized on the cachet of bookplates. Donors were actively engaged in the design of individualized bookplates for gifts of $10,000 and above. This process created an opportunity to honor or remember someone by personalizing a bookplate noting the gift. Involving the donor in bookplate design was a wonderful opportunity for library staff to get to know donors more personally.

Impact of Other Campaigns

As a former library development director once said, the effect of a larger campaign can be like a giant passing planet, pulling smaller astronomical bodies along with its strong gravitational field. During the five-year NEH campaign the library mounted several mini-campaigns (see descriptions below). At the time the NEH challenge began, the university-at-large was in the midst of its largest development campaign to date—the Campaign for Johns Hopkins. This campaign began before the NEH challenge started and ended before the NEH challenge was over. Both positive and negative effects resulted from having the library campaign overlap a larger institutional campaign. The benefits were principally a heightened awareness of fundraising throughout the university community, and an expanded central development staff available for assistance. The university's trustees, alumni, staff, and many friends shared a commitment to raising needed funds for the university. Money was invested to upgrade the university's fundraising information and donor tracking systems. Overall, the benefits to having two campaigns going on at the same time outweighed the difficulties.

Many of the difficulties from having the two campaigns running simultaneously stemmed from the university's organizational structure. Being a highly decentralized university has many advantages, but creates a fair amount of inefficient competition in certain arenas, such as fundraising. Because the NEH challenge began after the Campaign for Johns Hopkins started, each of the schools at Hopkins had fundraising plans in place and prospective donors identified. The library had no alumni base so it had to look hard at its traditional group of donors as well as elsewhere.

The campaign plan was clearly shaped by the timeline requirements placed on the university by NEH. Within the structure of its annual goals the library planned publicity, cultivation, solicitation, and ongoing stewardship. Soon after receiving word of the award from NEH, the library began to plan its prospect cultivation.

Year One

During the first year, a campaign committee of volunteers was established and chaired by a university trustee. This volunteer committee was initially useful for organizational reasons (e.g., review of potential major donor prospects), but the eventual solicitation of donors became more a task performed by university administrators than by volunteers. Other volunteer activities planned initially for this campaign committee were eventually taken over by the existing Library Advisory Council and the Friends Advisory Council.

A kickoff event for the campaign was held the first year and was combined with the celebration of the addition of the library's two millionth volume: *The History of the Baltimore Sun, 1937–1987*. The library received ample coverage of this event in the local media. Russell Baker, distinguished Hopkins alumnus and former *Sun* journalist, spoke, and lead campaign gifts were announced. A dinner was held afterward for 150 major prospects, and a direct mail solicitation followed to all current library donors.

Year Two

In the second year of the campaign, the library failed to reach its specified NEH goal and was given an extension of one additional year to meet the second target. (The campaign goal rose from $284,000 in the first year to $1,185,000 in the second year.) Several unanticipated events slowed progress in year two: (1) the library director of almost ten years left; (2) a large deficit in the School of Arts and Sciences necessitated a redirection of some prospects anticipated for library support; and (3) the university's president announced his retirement. On the positive side, membership in the Friends of the Libraries grew noticeably and the library's volunteer base expanded. The long-established Friends Advisory Council began to expand its functions to include a fundraising role. With the increased visibility of library needs, interest from alumni began growing. The class of 1939 established an endowment in support of the challenge. Also in year two, the library had to adjust its proposed spending plan in response to the actual cash accumulation anticipated. The campaign was receiving more pledges than originally projected, thus deferring the anticipated endowment income.

Year Two Extended

With a new library director on board, the second challenge goal was met at the end of the third year. During this period, fundraising for the challenge was back on track and moved ahead. One of the keys to success during this year was the establishment of a NEH endowment in honor of the university's retiring president. As a result, numerous university trustees and friends of the university were, for the first time, attracted to the NEH challenge grant campaign for the library. The initial response was over $300,000 in gifts or pledges in the former president's honor.

During this year, the library celebrated its twenty-fifth anniversary with a celebration featuring author Tom Wolfe as a guest speaker, and an academic convocation as the centerpiece. In conjunction with this event, a direct mail solicitation was made, producing a return of only $20,000. This reflected a return of only 0.7 percent of the mailing, which was sent to all of the 49,905 alumni of the Homewood Campus at Johns Hopkins. This year also saw an increase in giving to the Friends of the Libraries. Donations rose to $39,900 from the less than $20,000 in annual donations prior to the campaign. Alumni support continued to grow; the class of 1990 pledged $10,000 to create an endowment in support of the library challenge—a first for a graduating class.

This year also saw the increased commitment of the challenge's largest donor—a couple who were first attracted to the library because of the challenge grant. The gift level was raised to $500,000 and total challenge giving increased to almost $1,000,000. A significant, unexpected impact occurred when this donor decided to pledge an additional $1,500,000 to endow the position of library director. (This gift did not count toward the challenge grant.)

Year Three

The goal of $1,382,000 for challenge year three was the highest of all four years. The successful momentum of the prior year carried through to this year, and this goal was met and even slightly exceeded. The library's major donor continued an extraordinary giving pattern with a gift of over $500,000 to the campaign. An anonymous donor also came forward with a pledge of $200,000, and the support in honor of the university's retiring president continued, but at a lower level than the previous year. Plans continued to solicit gifts of $10,000 and above from remaining campaign prospects who were principally current or past members of the Library Advisory Council. Membership growth in the Friends of the Libraries continued, with a total membership nearing one thousand for the year. Notable among the year's activities was an effort by the Friends, as part of its sixtieth anniversary celebration, to raise money in support of the challenge grant. This year also saw the expansion of the library development office with the addition of an assistant director of library development.

The Final Year

The goal for year four was $1,149,000. Not only was this goal met, thus completing the challenge, but an additional $210,000 was raised in response to the challenge. Five gifts in excess of $100,000 were received. The library's largest donor again contributed over $500,000, and also stimulated more giving by providing an anonymous dollar-for-dollar match of all gifts to the challenge grant during the last six months of the campaign. This end-of-the-campaign match was announced at a benefit concert of Cole Porter music, which earned some $6,000 for the humanities endowment and brought nearly six hundred persons to the program. To determine how successful this six-month campaign was, a comparison was made with the same six-month period in the spring of 1991, when the library mounted a sixtieth anniversary of the Friends campaign to raise funds. The analysis revealed that the impact of the dollar-for-dollar match was dramatic: (1) giving increased sixfold; (2) the total number of donors increased more than threefold; and (3) the number of donors giving between $1,000 and $5,000 increased nearly fivefold. A gift annuity of $300,000 and a $260,000 gift-in-kind were also received in response to this match. This dollar-for-dollar match at the end of the campaign ensured the success of the challenge grant and pushed fundraising over the top.

The library celebrated the successful completion of the challenge grant with a reception for major donors hosted by the university's president. The Friends of the Libraries also celebrated the campaign's success at their first program in the fall of 1992.

Impact on Humanities Support

Being an endowment campaign built over a five-year period, the NEH challenge has generated a gradual but steady increase in endowment yield for humanities materials spending. In fiscal year 1993–1994, the anticipated payout on the new endowment was over $330,000. Earnings increased after fiscal year 1993–1994 as trust and bequest funds were added to the principal. The overall result of the new NEH endowment has been almost a doubling of endowment income for library materials. The stability created for humanities acquisitions funding has been enormous.

The effect of such financial stability on the humanities collection has been great. Johns Hopkins, a comparatively small university, has only eighty-six faculty in the humanities. Those faculty must be able to design broad disciplinary and multidisciplinary courses that reflect the shifting and often multidisciplinary directions of their fields and of their research. Because of their small number and the breadth of study offered, faculty must be able to effect curricular change rapidly. These characteristics of Johns Hopkins require, in turn, rich and highly responsive library collections. Perhaps the most important impact of the NEH challenge grant has been the library's strengthened ability to respond to these critical needs of humanities faculty.

Impact on Library Fundraising Capabilities

The year before the five-year NEH challenge grant campaign began, the library raised a total of $425,815 from 820 donors. In the final year of the challenge grant, the library raised over $2.8 million in qualifying and nonqualifying gifts from 1,691 donors. The library's donor base was doubled and the giving level increased nearly sevenfold. Much of the improvement in library fundraising is attributable to the NEH challenge grant, including: (1) an increase in Friends membership by 50 percent; (2) for the first time, establishment of the trustee-led Library Advisory Council as an effective fundraising body; and (3) the ability to return repeatedly to friends over the last five years, and to receive a dependable and generous response.

The year after the challenge grant ended was a challenge of another sort. The university began gearing up for another major campaign and the library was again behind several Hopkins schools charging out of the blocks. Although gifts received by the library did fall off, as expected in this first year after the campaign, the principal development focus was to minimize the loss of the newly gained momentum from the success of the NEH challenge.

The library also proved it could plan and deliver high-visibility fundraising events. While some might argue that such events do not produce much direct economic return in relation to the enormous effort required to mount them, there are clearly other benefits. The attention the library receives has a high immediate and longer-term value. These types of events can be seen as a form of cultivation of donors or investment in development, which bring returns over a longer time period. Well-engineered events also provide excellent opportunities to thank major donors, and are important internally for maintaining support from both university officials and volunteers.

Impact on Future Fundraising Efforts

In addition to building strength for the humanities collections, the challenge grant has positioned the library well for the next campaign. Without the foundation provided by this successful campaign, it would be difficult to convince university administrators and friends that a new campaign goal for the library of $20 to $25 million is possible. The next university campaign began in late 1994 and will carry to the edge of the next century.

6 Tulsa Library Trust

CATHY AUDLEY AND PAT WOODRUM

In just over a decade, Tulsa City-County Library's (TCCL) endowment fund grew from $13,970 to nearly $5,000,000. This growth was bolstered by donations from businesses, foundations, families, and the National Endowment for the Humanities (NEH). The invested principal now generates enough annual income to fund: the purchase of thousands of new books, videos, cassettes, and compact discs; a children's summer reading program; two distinguished author awards; a variety of library events; new equipment and databases; volunteer and staff recognition awards; an adult literacy service; and numerous other library enhancements.

This is the story of how a vision became a reality—a tale of community pride, volunteer involvement, and personalized fundraising. Tulsa's experience is a success story that has been and can be duplicated by libraries of all sizes across the country. The strategy has been tried and proved. And, for the TCCL, the resulting rewards have created a synergism that extends far beyond monetary value. Library leaders who are willing to set a goal and commit to blending enthusiasm with hard work and perseverance can adapt Tulsa's techniques to write their own stories of success.

Let us take you back to the beginning. In 1972, members of TCCL's commission and Friends of the Library had the foresight to

Cathy Audley is trust manager and Pat Woodrum is executive director of the Tulsa City-County library system in Tulsa, Oklahoma.

join together to create a third entity, the Tulsa Library Trust. The trust was founded expressly for the purpose of receiving and administering contributions to and for the benefit of the library, and for the advancement of literature and library science. It was set up as a public foundation under Section 501(c)(3) of the Internal Revenue Code so that donors could make tax-deductible gifts, transfers, or bequests of cash, stock, or property to the library. A five-member board was established. The bylaws designated that two members were to be appointed by the library commission, two members selected by the Friends, and a fifth member was to be mutually agreed upon by both groups. Later, the board was increased to seven members.

When the trust was created, only $10 was deposited in its account; two years later its assets were $250. In 1976, following the untimely death of Allie Beth Martin, then director of the TCCL system and president of the American Library Association, a total of $9,000 in donations was received to set up a scholarship fund for library science students in her memory. Over the next few years, other small memorial contributions and unsolicited gifts were deposited into this fund. By the summer of 1980, the fund's account balance was $13,970. An aggressive effort to secure donations had not yet been made.

In 1980, as staff and volunteers began to plan for a community-wide celebration of the TCCL system's twentieth anniversary, many watched with concern as some of the nation's libraries faced severe financial trouble. Public libraries from California to the East Coast were being forced to sharply curtail their acquisitions, reduce hours of service, lay off personnel, and eliminate programs. Although TCCL's operating funds, which are derived from property taxes, were adequate to meet current needs, no one knew what the future might hold. The anniversary presented an opportune time to combine a celebration of the past with an effort to seek additional funding sources that would assure a bright and secure future for the library system.

Developing an Endowment

Based on a proposal from library staff, the trust board and the library commission adopted a goal to develop the endowment.

The trust was already in existence and an endowment would provide both an "insurance policy" to safeguard against possible threats to survival, and ongoing income that would allow the library to dedicate itself to moving toward an even higher level of performance.

The head of the library's public relations department was assigned the added responsibilities of part-time development officer to work with the library executive director and volunteers in researching, organizing, and implementing a campaign. The first step was to conduct a feasibility study. A literature search and letters and calls of inquiry to a number of public libraries revealed that the few endowments already in place had been created primarily by bequests. New York Public Library alone was fully involved in a longstanding development effort. The executive director and public relations manager then called on fifteen to twenty local business and civic leaders to gauge their support of an endowment drive for the Tulsa library and to ask for advice. The response was favorable; all agreed that creating an endowment was a good idea, yet several cautioned that it might be hard to sell because the library was a tax-supported institution. The community leaders also shared suggestions for effective fundraising methods and described techniques used by other organizations. The visits yielded a list of potential contributors and an indication of how much money could be raised in Tulsa. In some cases the visit was the community leader's first introduction to the library and its services. The individuals contacted expressed pleasure in the fact that their advice was being sought on the project *before* it took shape. They were also impressed that the librarians made personal visits.

At that time, the trust board members had little or no fundraising experience, so they formed a trust development committee of seven—two oil executives, two bankers, a former mayor, an attorney, and a local philanthropist who was a longtime library commissioner. The members were all respected for their giving patterns and for their knowledge of fundraising practices.

A list of potential contributors (foundations and corporations) was prepared from numerous sources and reviewed by the committee. Using information compiled on each potential contributor such as total assets, number of employees, past community contributions, and the advice of committee members, committee members projected the amount to solicit from each prospect. The projected campaign goal totaled $1 million, yet the development committee reasoned that donors often figure their donations as a percentage of the campaign goal; therefore, the total was doubled and the group set an optimistic goal of $2 million to be raised in pledges over a three-to-five-year period.

Brief consideration was given to working with a professional fundraising firm. After talking with groups that had used such consultants, however, the committee decided that a sincere, low-key approach would be more effective in this situation than a high-pressure campaign coordinated by people from outside the organization.

A case statement was written to outline the library's mission and its vision for the future. The case explained, "Today's public library faces unique challenges. It must be prepared to respond with vigor, enthusiasm and expertise to the ever changing and expanding information and resource needs of a complex, fast-paced, industrialized society." The statement went on to enumerate the potential uses of interest from the endowment fund. Proposed projects ranged from strengthening specific materials collections to expanding the adult literacy service and establishing a program series featuring nationally renowned authors.

The Anniversary Celebration

A publicity and marketing plan was devised using two simultaneous approaches. One approach was a series of personalized VIP breakfast tours of the central library for prospective donors and the other was a seven-month-long community celebration of the twentieth anniversary of the library system.

About one hundred volunteers were recruited to help the staff create and carry out a celebration that would involve the entire community and heighten public awareness of the library's resources and services. The theme "Happy Birthday Library and Many Happy Returns" was chosen to encompass the fundraising endeavor. The anniversary committee accomplished the following:

Prepared a multimedia slide show depicting the library's history and presented it to community groups

Ran a six-week mystery contest on a local radio station with clues that could only be found in a library. The winner received a $1,000 check from the broadcasting company.

Presented public service spots on radio and television stations

Hosted a birthday party at each of the twenty-one library facilities

Featured twenty-one Oklahoma authors in programs at each library

Designed and conducted a children's summer reading program based on the birthday theme

Sponsored a three-day storytelling festival

Conducted oral history interviews with people who were instrumental in the library's development

Found a benefactor and commissioned an artist to produce a multimedia collage depicting the library's history

Worked with a local television station to produce a prime-time, thirty-minute special about the library

Secured a contribution to write and publish an eighty-page history of the library

Established a library hall of fame and inducted the initial members

Presented a series of six events at as many libraries, featuring internationally known authors

Offered numerous public programs, including cooking demonstrations, to highlight special collections of the library.

While all of this was going on and the library was attracting a great deal of media attention, foundation trustees and chief executive officers of corporations were being invited to attend the personalized VIP breakfast tours of the central library. The development committee had decided to focus its efforts on securing large donations of $10,000 to $100,000 to be pledged over three to five years.

VIP Breakfast Tours

The development team, composed of the library commissioner, the public relations manager who was now also identified as the trust manager, and the executive director, hosted the VIP breakfast tours that were conceived as the primary fundraising strategy. Following is an account of how they worked.

The library commissioner, who was a social friend of most of the VIPs, personally called the guests and invited them to join her for breakfast and a tour of the library on a specific date. Four to six VIPs were invited for each tour. They were asked to arrive at 8 AM, promised that only one-and-one-half hours would be taken from their schedules, and were given directions to a special parking area. The invitation was confirmed in writing.

Before the tour, the trust manager researched library resources and made confidential calls to secretaries, spouses, or others close to the VIPs to gather personal information that would help the staff select examples of library services and materials of personal interest to the guests. She noted their alma maters, hobbies, family members, travel destinations, volunteer and business activities, and so on. Staff members prepared and rehearsed their segments of the tour according to a minute-by-minute schedule.

When the VIPs arrived on the appointed date, a security guard greeted them, unlocked the library door (the library opens at 9 AM), and directed them to the fourth floor conference room. There they joined the library commissioner, executive director, and trust manager for a light breakfast. Library cards for each VIP were used as place cards. Conversation was quickly turned to the library's history, and its organization, leadership, and role in the community. An eight-minute slide-tape show depicted library services.

The group then began a walking tour of the library. In each department of the library, guests were introduced to the department manager who had been briefed in advance and had prepared a concise presentation appealing to the guests' personal interests, while illustrating the department's collections and services. For example, a VIP's name or company was the subject of an online database search. A topographical map shown to the group just happened to have the location of a guest's lake home on it. A medical directory was opened to a photo of another's physician son. The children's department issued a library card for a recently born grandchild. Books and vertical files on the country a guest was getting ready to visit were highlighted. If guests were golf or classical music enthusiasts, a golf video and a classical CD would be playing when the group walked through the media center. Library escorts also sprinkled the tour with human interest stories of library use and impressive facts and statistics.

The tour concluded near the library entrance where participants stopped briefly for another cup of coffee. They were given packets of information and were told about the trust, the library's needs for the future, and the fundraising goal. After questions and answers, the library commissioner closed by saying that the trust manager would be calling next week to make appointments for the three-member development team to visit them at their offices. Immediately following the VIP tour, a letter was sent to the guests thanking them for taking time from their busy schedules to attend the VIP tour. Approximately two weeks later, the development team met with the potential contributor, restated the library's need, and asked for a donation of a specific amount, which could be pledged over a three-to-five-year period or at the discretion of the donor. Several contributors requested a written follow-up. Others made their pledges on the spot.

The results were incredible. Within a twelve-month period, $1.1 million was raised in pledges. But the monetary rewards were only part of what was gained for the library. At the end of the fiscal year following the anniversary celebration, circulation statistics showed a record increase of 15 percent. In addition, a good working relationship was developed with leaders of the corporate community. Some had never been inside any of the Tulsa public libraries prior to the VIP breakfasts. Many began to send their employees to the library and the level of activity increased so rapidly in the business and technology department that another staff member was added.

Occasionally, the VIPs sent thank-you notes for having been invited to the tours. One wrote, "It was the best example of perfect salesmanship followed by a magnificent job of merchandising . . . I came away with a great determination to help you in whatever you are attempting to do." Librarians were happily surprised when they read an article in a national magazine about another CEO of a major Tulsa corporation. It said, "Give him a chance to talk about . . . the public library system. He'll gladly bend your ear."

The Next Initiatives

The grand finale of the anniversary celebration was a formal dinner for about 350 persons on the main floor of the central library, with George Plimpton as the keynote speaker. Major contributors to the trust were invited to be the library's guests and were presented with plaques of appreciation at a private reception with Mr. Plimpton before the dinner. These contributors were also recognized in a printed program and from the podium during dinner.

The Tulsa Library Trust had achieved just over half of its $2 million goal when the oil bust hit Oklahoma. The local economy was suddenly on the decline and many of the businesses still on the prospect list found themselves facing a fragile financial position. The development committee decided to temporarily downplay its efforts, regroup, and consider alternative fundraising strategies.

The trust launched a new phase in its endowment campaign when it applied for and was awarded a challenge grant from the

NEH. The purpose of the grant was to create a $1 million endowment earmarked for humanities collections, services, and programs. If $750,000 in first-time local contributions could be secured over a three-year period, NEH would match them with $250,000. This was the impetus needed to jump-start the campaign.

In the summer of 1984 the trust received its largest single contribution—$600,000 from a family with whom the executive director and a supporter had been fostering a relationship for several months. A news conference was held and, in appreciation of the donors, the library commission renamed a new regional library for the couple. Shortly thereafter, VIP tours were reactivated, additional development volunteers became involved, and the trust hosted a VIP tea for women targeted as potential contributors. Gradually, the remaining $150,000 needed for the NEH match was raised, mostly in donations of $500 to $5,000.

In the interim, the library trust created a Distinguished Author Award to be given annually to an author of prominent literary distinction whose body of work had made a significant contribution to the field of literature and letters. The winner comes to Tulsa to receive the award and to speak at a black-tie dinner in the central library on a Friday evening and at a free public program the next morning. At the inaugural dinner in December 1985, a surprise announcement was made that the award would hereafter be named the Peggy V. Helmerich Distinguished Author Award in honor of the library commissioner who was the key volunteer on the development team.

The Helmerich Award celebrated its tenth anniversary in 1994 and is regarded as a gift to the community as well as a preeminent social event in Tulsa. Winners include Saul Bellow, John Updike, Toni Morrison, John le Carre, Norman Mailer, and Eudora Welty. The award is also an effective cultivation activity that annually involves about ninety volunteers as members of a planning committee; these volunteers represent donors and potential donors who may not otherwise have participated in library events. Media publicity about the award and related events (book reviews, exhibits, film showings, panel presentations about the author, and the induction of new TCCL hall of fame members during the dinner) is plentiful and draws attention to the library trust. In fact, the library contracted with a clipping service one year and received news stories about the award from 126 papers in the United States and Canada. The dinner attracts about 450 guests; $85 per plate tickets are sold out well in advance. The invitations include an RSVP card that offers the option, "____ I cannot attend, but I am enclosing a contribution to the Tulsa Library Trust." This alone produces several thousand dollars in donations.

The response from both authors and Tulsans to the Helmerich Award was so exceptional that the trust manager and executive director invited another family to endow an award for authors of children's and young adults' books. This was established in 1991 as the Anne V. Zarrow Award for Young People's Literature and has been given to authors S. E. Hinton, Madeleine L'Engle, Katherine Paterson, and Lois Lowry. The main event in this case is not a black-tie dinner, but rather a Friday evening family event with punch and cookies.

The author's appearance comes at the climax of the children's summer reading program, in which participation has more than doubled since the trust began funding it in 1982. Now, more than twenty-eight thousand children read to earn rewards in the summer program.

In the years immediately following the completion of the fund drive for the NEH challenge grant, pledges continued to be paid, but the trust slowed aggressive private fundraising activities while the system and its supporters concentrated on an all-out campaign to promote passage of a $4.2 million bond issue and a one-mill increase in annual property tax revenue for library operations. Both issues won record-breaking votes of approval from the people of Tulsa County in August 1988.

Donor Incentives

Meanwhile, donor cultivation activities were ongoing. Two of these are most notable:

> The library took advantage of as many opportunities as possible to maintain contact with trust donors. They were mailed invitations, annual reports, copies of editorials, Christmas cards, and so on, and were added to the Friends of the Library group. Individuals were also called upon to serve as speakers and on advisory committees when appropriate.

> In recognition of Mrs. Helmerich's dedication to building the endowment, the executive director and trust manager nominated her for several awards, all of which she won. She was named the country's Outstanding Philanthropist of the Year by the National Society of Fund Raising Executives, and

was the recipient of the American Library Association's Trustee Citation, the Oklahoma Library Association's Citizen's Recognition Award, and the Medici Award presented by the Tulsa Ballet Theatre.

In 1990, the library trust received a pledge that topped even the largest single contribution of $600,000—this time it was from the Helmerich family for $750,000. Mr. Helmerich designated that a portion of the gift be used to endow the Helmerich Award and double the cash honorarium to $20,000. In honor of the family's generosity and Mrs. Helmerich's gifts of time and talent, the library commission named its newest branch the Peggy V. Helmerich Library when it opened in 1991.

Although the library encourages nonearmarked gifts to the general or humanities endowments, corporate donations are sought to fund high-visibility special projects. Also, individual givers who have a special interest are invited to create an endowment large enough to perpetually fund collections or services. For instance, a donor who had a longtime concern about illiteracy recently pledged $100,000 to endow the Adult Literacy Service, which has been renamed in her honor.

Corporate sponsorships for annual programs usually endure from year to year because the businesses receive valuable recognition and publicity for their goodwill, and a strong bond develops between the library and corporate people who work together to assure successful programs. Library trust projects funded by corporate sponsors include: the Teen Team, a summer volunteer force of thirteen- to fifteen-year-olds; the Run to Read, an eight-kilometer road race and fundraiser for the literacy service; the Summer Reading Program drawing for more than seventy-five prizes (including a trip for a family of four) for children who complete the program; and a Read to Succeed motivation program for at-risk middle-school students.

As the Tulsa Library Trust implements numerous trust-funded programs, projects, and events, it continues to seek gifts and cultivate new donors in an effort to accomplish an always-expanding vision for the future. The current five-year development plan calls for:

A campaign to raise an additional $4 million for the endowment

Implementation of a tribute giving program

Development of a sophisticated donor database

Organization of an annual giving program

Initiation of planned giving solicitation strategies.

The lessons learned and the philosophies engendered by the creation of the Tulsa Library Trust's endowment are many. The time-honored maxim of "success breeds success" was validated repeatedly by the trust's experience. One of the best-demonstrated assertions is that library leaders have the responsibility to offer people "the opportunity to give." The words of novelist and satirist Anatole France provide perhaps the clearest summation, "To accomplish great things, we must not only act, but also dream, not only plan, but also believe."

7 # The Role of Special Collections in Library Development

VICTORIA STEELE

My perspective on the role of special collections in library development is somewhat unusual. I have been both a director of development and the head of special collections *in* a major university research library. I can therefore offer views from both sides of the tall fence that often separates librarians from fundraisers. In addition to my direct experience, I consult on fundraising, sometimes at the invitation of librarians wanting to improve their relationships with development staff and sometimes at the invitation of fundraisers hoping to strengthen their dealings with librarians.

In the first part of this chapter, I comment generally on this experience; that is, I provide a conceptual overview of how development, in my judgment, works best and how special collections fit into that framework. Following this general discussion, I offer specifics on what development people want from special collections librarians and what special collections people want from development staff. In the last part of the chapter, I focus on an institution-specific fundraising event, the Scripter Awards at the University of Southern California Libraries, as an example of the challenges and

Victoria Steele is the head of the Department of Special Collections at the University of Southern California Libraries. A different version of this chapter appeared as "Of Sherpas and Mountain Climbers" in *Rare Books and Manuscripts Librarianship* 9, no. 2 (1994).

opportunities of fundraising in an academic environment—and of the role of special collections therein.

Overview

The key to a successful library fundraising program is a synergistic relationship between development professionals and librarians. Development staff cannot succeed without the creative input of librarians, and librarians cannot achieve their vision without the practical assistance of talented fundraisers. When either side of the partnership is weak, results are mediocre, and the program can actually *lose* money. Though some workplace relationships can survive imbalances, development is not one of them.

The pivotal figure in any library fundraising effort is the library director. As I stress at length elsewhere, successful fundraising depends on the leadership and participation of the library director, who provides the energy, drive, and momentum for the fundraising effort. (Steele and Elder 1992) Fundraising campaigns can be sustained without fundraisers, but they cannot be sustained without a library leader.

The additional participation of special collections librarians in the development program can be an enormous boost to a fundraising effort. Special collections librarians can, for instance, do the following:

Provide continuity to the development program during periods of leadership change

Attract and broaden the interests of collectors in the library

Relieve the library director of full responsibility for keeping relationships with donors and prospects alive

Contribute, through exhibits and programming, to the intellectual and cultural vitality of the library

Add to the brainpower of the development effort.

A library director and a head of special collections who share a commitment to fundraising can be a formidable force for library development. Supported by talented development staff, the library director and head of special collections can have spectacular success. Where such partnerships exist, they should be treasured.

Sadly, however, such partnerships are rare. People who are naturally gifted fundraisers are not plentiful in this world; and, in libraries, those people who *are* naturally talented fundraisers may not be in the critical positions of library director or head of special collections. Moreover, development staff and librarians often do not understand how they can best work together. This last point merits fuller comment.

Sherpa Guides and Mountain Climbers

Development works best when librarians see themselves as leading the fundraising expedition and development staff understand themselves to be in the role of guides. In other words, librarians are like mountain climbers and development officers are like Sherpas.

No aspersion is intended by comparing development professionals to Sherpas. On the contrary, the implication is that Sherpas know the way up the mountain and keep us from making fatal mistakes. High-stakes fundraising, like high-altitude climbing, is a collaborative undertaking, and all its participants are valuable and essential to achieving the ultimate goal. The key is to keep the roles distinct. Just as a Sherpa's job is to show his charges how to get safely to the top of a mountain, so a fundraiser's job is to help a library director meet, get to know, and effectively solicit major-donor prospects.

Unfortunately, however, we often see the development officer-Sherpa guide *assuming* the role of librarian-mountain climber. Such a blurring of roles can result from the library director's delegating the fundraising responsibility to development staff because he or she does not want to do it, from the development officer's taking on the fundraising responsibility because the library director is not good at it, or from their just not realizing that their roles should be distinct. Whatever the cause, blurred roles lead to lackluster results.

There are several reasons this is so. For one, when cultivating prospects, we must realize that donors and potential donors want to have relationships with people in positions of authority and prestige. *Money wants to talk to power.* No matter how likeable, effective, or attractive they may be, development people generally do not hold line positions in libraries. Whatever their title, they are staff. Though the library director will certainly listen to the counsel of the trusted Sherpa during their ascent, it must be the library director who plants the flag on the summit.

Another reason is that fundraisers who try to substitute for the library director often begin to think of themselves as mountain climbers—as the lead figures in the development effort —and consequently begin to feel that essential Sherpa tasks are beneath their concern. Trying to fill someone else's role, they cease to play their own. This scenario leads to disaster for the development program.

Finally, the very fact that fundraisers *are* fundraisers tends to scare prospective donors away. When it comes time to ask for a gift, the donor will likely be not only more flattered, but also more relaxed if a librarian makes the request. However congenial, the fundraiser is too identifiably a person with a motive, a person who will be seen as having the job of separating donors from their money. Hence, even when donors may be ready to give, they tend to be on their guard against fundraisers.

Librarians, then, should think in terms of managing relationships with donors, rather than thinking that fundraisers will manage the relationships by proxy. At the same time, since development can be time consuming, it behooves the director to focus his or her energies on prospects who have the greatest potential, leaving relationships that either still need to grow, or show less potential, to other librarians. Here, special collections librarians can be invaluable. They can identify and initially cultivate a donor and, at the right time, introduce the donor to the library director and the development director. Depending on the situation and the prospect's potential, the library director might then take the lead and eventually make the solicitation. Or, if the time is not ripe for a solicitation, the best strategy might be to let the special collections librarian continue to foster the relationship, while keeping the library director and development officer informed.

A Formidable Fundraising Duo

Earlier I said that the head of special collections and the library director can make a formidable fundraising duo if they share a commitment to development. Essentially, the head of special collections can become a deputy fundraiser, relieving the director of some of the load of a busy program. (Unfortunately, the scenario in which the head of special collections is a more talented and experienced fundraiser than the library director is a common one. *Becoming a Fundraiser* was written partially in an attempt to address this particular problem.) With the special collections librarian assuming an active role, the library director will not have to make every call and attend every event. The library director will also be able to count on the head of special collections to cultivate and solicit prospects in a way that will be most beneficial to the overall program and to the strategic goals of the library, instead of isolating prospects for narrow opportunities that will benefit special collections alone. The library director will be able to depend as well on the special collections head to be attentive to donor relations, to such things as follow-up letters and calls—activities whose importance is best appreciated and understood by librarians fully invested in development.

For all of these reasons and more, special collections people who are good at development can be extremely valuable to a fundraising program. They can sustain a program when it is flagging. They can help new library directors develop comfort with fundraising. They can help donors make the transition to new leadership and ensure their continued commitment to the library. They can also try to keep the development staff focused on strategic goals.

Fundraising Essentials: Uniqueness, Niche, and Ethics

Once librarians and fundraisers understand their different roles, they need to understand their library's uniqueness and niche, and to have a firm grasp of fundraising ethics.

Each library, institution, donor, director, and fundraiser is unique. Therefore, what works in one institution may not work in another (an important point for readers of this book who are considering adopting strategies or techniques used in one institution to their own). The uniqueness principle accounts for why one institution can raise money and another, using more or less the same methods, cannot. It also accounts for why strategies that have worked well at one time for an institution may not work well later on, when the unique individuals responsible for them are no longer part of the organization. Uniqueness applies as well to donors: what works for one may not work for another. The uniqueness principle, in brief, accounts for the fragility of development programs: ones that are successful have a cluster of unique, positive elements; ones that are not have lost or lack some aspect or aspects of the positive mix.

An organization's uniqueness intersects with its purposes, creating a niche that belongs to it alone. An understanding of niche helps librarians and fundraisers characterize the library's goals effectively, a key activity in fundraising. Just as important, it helps librarians make decisions about accepting money or collections. Librarians have to make clear to fundraisers that gifts should dovetail with the library's aims and existing holdings. This matter can cause friction between special collections librarians and development staff, who may want librarians to accept inappropriate collections in hopes of eventually obtaining funds from their contributors. Not only is such baiting a poor management tactic, not only does it tax the library's staff and resources with no certain benefit in return, but it is ethically dubious as well.

As for fundraising ethics, the general principle is that development should seek consonance between a donor's wishes and a library's needs, and it should proceed in an open and balanced way. A fundraising program can be considered to be successful when it results in gifts that contribute to the strategic vision for the library. A program is *not* successful when it results in gifts that are, in fact, tangential, distracting, or come with cumbersome strings attached. A principled, ethical approach to fundraising frees participants to go forward with enthusiasm, confident that their actions are both honorable and in the best interests of the institution.

The Development Team

The most effective way to use a head of special collections, provided the head is a mountain climber, is to put him or her on the development team and treat the collections head much as you would a valuable volunteer. As a team member, he or she will attend regular development meetings which are run by the development staff and in which the library director participates. The head of special collections will contribute items to the agenda, make suggestions about priorities and direction for the program, and help to develop individual donor strategies.

The head of special collections can also play an important role in the management of the Friends and Friends board. Often, the special collections head and the library director are the two librarians who are continuing ad hoc members of the board, and reports from both are always key agenda items for board meetings. Other librarians or library staff make guest appearances at board meetings as appropriate. As a member of the board, the head of special collections can work with the development staff to focus the board's attention on big-picture issues and fundraising, not operational matters or micro-level purchases. Assuming that the library director is not involved in planning board meeting agendas, and that the development staff does do not always have detailed knowledge of specific library issues, the head of special collections can be helpful in keeping the right messages in front of Friends' board members. He or she can also help with the all-important activity of recruiting the highest-level prospects to serve on the board.

The Sherpa aspects of running the Friends should be left to development staff. They attend to event management, membership maintenance, minutes preparation, and the like, knowing they make the best use of the head of special collections in the role of a mountain climber.

What Development People Want from Special Collections

Development people long to work with librarians who know how to present a good image and whose personal style, demeanor, and manners are impeccable. They want to have meetings in offices that convey an air of competence and professionalism and in which the choice of personal touches is dignified and appropriate.

Development people treasure librarians with good verbal communication skills. They delight in—and will use constantly—librarians who can give a tour of their operation that is brief and that communicates infectious enthusiasm. They look for someone who is comfortable with personal contact, who is a good listener, and who can connect with donors and prospects. They appreciate librarians who have a sense of occasion and who feel at home fulfilling ceremonial functions. They value librarians who can modify their style to communicate their message with optimum effectiveness. Development people are grateful to work with librarians who are secure enough to be able to accept gentle coaching about what to say, how to say it, and when to say it.

Development people equally prize written communication skills. The librarian who can write an artful or compelling letter or proposal is invaluable to development staff. Most development people view proposal writing as a collaborative process: they expect librarians to supply the basic facts and rationale for a proposal that they then translate into a persuasive, carefully crafted and packaged presentation. But the more input they have from librarians, and the more clearly librarians can articulate their vision and the impact funding would have on that vision, the more able development staff are to respond to development opportunities.

Development people hope to work with special collections librarians who understand how development works. They appreciate librarians who realize that it is *they* who must ask collectors and other prospects for monetary gifts, including processing funds. Development people do not want to be asked to make a plea for money after a gift-in-kind has been made.

Development people also want to work with librarians who are realistic about what needs are fundable: retrospective conversion, small facilities improvements, and the purchase of supplies and equipment may not be appealing to donors. Development staff hope to be fed information about viable prospects, not "vague others" (people who are not known to you or your organization and are unlikely to have any interest in it) or busybodies (small-time donors who command and expect the attentions normally given to major-gift prospects). In terms of events, development people want to work with librarians who will help them create occasions that are fun and interesting to a wide variety of donors and donor prospects. Though recognizing the value of events that may cater to a small number of rare book and manuscript enthusiasts, development people know that generally these cannot be the center of an effective program.

Finally, development people are grateful to a librarian who displays a willingness to fully participate in events —a librarian who will meet and greet, work the crowd, be an effective host, and even volunteer to tackle a Sherpa-ish task if necessary.

What Special Collections People Want from Development

More than anything else, special collections people want to work with development people who understand the Sherpa-mountain climber relationship. Special collections librarians (and other librarians) react indignantly when development people act as though librarians are subordinate to development. They are not. In forging a good relationship with special collections librarians, it is very important that development officers be clear about who is assisting whom. They need to manage their relationships with special collections librarians with a care and finesse such that special collections people become so deeply committed to fundraising that they *willingly* offer to assist the process and agree to climb the mountains that the development people suggest they climb.

One of the ways development people can foster the cooperation of special collections librarians is by keeping them briefed and involved in development, much as they do the library director. They should also provide the fundraising-savvy special collections librarian with some of the same services they give to the library director, such as ghosting follow-up letters and speeches.

Special collections people appreciate development people who are intelligent and creative and who have excellent verbal and written communication skills. They want to work with development staff capable of creating development literature that will be a credit to their library. They want to work with development officers who can define development goals (such as strengthening volunteer leadership) and create action plans to realize those goals. Perhaps most important, they want to work with fundraisers who appreciate libraries, are well educated, and have intellectual agility and depth. They want to work with fundraisers who appreciate that the issues facing libraries may differ from those facing athletic departments, and that prospective donors to libraries have interests that differ from those who contribute to a fund for, say, football scholarships.

Special collections librarians resent being pressured to accept collections that are not appropriate or do not align with their institutional niche. Special collections librarians are constantly trying to prevent their departments from becoming the institutional equivalent of a garage, attic, or toxic waste site. Thus, their vigilance, rather than cooperation, will be activated when they are approached to accept questionable gifts-in-kind.

Neither do special collections librarians want to be told, with little or no warning, to prepare special exhibits for cultivation or recognition purposes. Exhibits, though they can be excellent development tools, are very time-consuming and are generally scheduled with long lead times, so that often overworked staffs can prepare them, while still attending to public service duties. If, however, the head of special collections is a member of the development team, and thus fully committed to the program's goals, he or she may *offer* to see that an exhibit is done because of its value to the larger enterprise. When it comes to exhibits, the latter strategy of involvement and commitment is much more effective than the former.

Finally, special collections people want to work with talented and successful fundraisers. They will be happy to associate themselves with a development team that strives for, and achieves, excellence.

Let us turn now to a concrete example of fundraising in action and the role of special collections therein.

The Scripter Award

Since 1988, the Friends of the University of Southern California Libraries have sponsored the Scripter Award, an award honoring the "best realization of a book as film." The award goes to two people: the author of a book on which a film is based and the screenwriter who adapted the book to the screen. Eligible films based on books (of which there are approximately thirty each year) are identified and screenings are arranged for a high-level selection committee, a group that includes writers, key people in the film industry, and several members of the Friends' board. Selection committee members are also expected to read each of the original books adapted to the screen.

The award allows the University of Southern California Libraries to build a bridge between itself, representing books and authors, and Hollywood, representing films and screenwriters. It has other purposes as well: (1) to raise money for the library's endowment, (2) to take advantage of the library's special niche by creating a giving opportunity that is attractive to members of the Los Angeles community, and (3) to increase the visibility of the library's development efforts in several target constituencies.

The Scripter Awards are presented at a black-tie dinner held in the main library's stately reference room. A tremendous effort is made to ensure that winning writers are present and that as many stars, directors, producers, and studio executives as possible are in attendance. The evening is orchestrated with such care that it could virtually be televised: film clips, music, lighting, and star presenters provide guests with maximum entertainment value. Some of the celebrities who have been associated with the Scripter Awards are Anne Archer, Anne Bancroft, Shari Belafonte, Dixie Carter, Geena Davis, Diane Ladd, Marjorie Lord, Penny Marshall, Steven Spielberg, and Robin Williams. Since the beginning, all the work associated with the event (e.g., communicating with the winners, obtaining celebrity guests, staging the evening) has been done in-house by a small group of people: one or two development staff, the head of special collections, the assistant to the head of special collections, and the facilities manager.

To date, Scripter-winning books/films are:

1988	*84 Charing Cross Road*
1989	*The Accidental Tourist*
1990	*Awakenings*
1991	*Fried Green Tomatoes*
1992	*A River Runs through It*
1993	*Schindler's List*
1994	*The Shawshank Redemption*

As the head of special collections at the University of Southern California, I have played an active role in the Scripter Awards and gala. I have served on the selection committee, so that I have had the opportunity to interact with prospects at screenings. I have also participated in the work of the event committee, the group that sells tickets and makes minor decisions about the look and style of the event. I have solicited individuals to underwrite the event and have asked others to purchase tables (at $2,500, $5,000, and $10,000, depending on location in the room) and to buy individual tickets (at $250 each). On the evening itself, I work the crowd during the reception and, at dinner, host a table of carefully selected prospects.

If these are active mountain-climbing tasks, I have also performed innumerable Sherpa-like tasks for the Scripter Award. I have helped orchestrate the evening by planning the order of events, writing speeches for various presenters, advising on which prospects should be seated at which tables, writing copy for the program, working with publicists, and so on. Being invested in the success of the event, I have volunteered to help with Sherpa-ish aspects of its management.

My assistant has been involved in many ways also. For example, she has been responsible for compiling the video montage of the titles of the eligible films, the five finalists, and the winning film that opens the evening's program. She has also supervised the complex move of books, tables, and chairs out of the reference room for the event and their move back in again, so that public service can resume. And, among additional tasks, she has prepared special exhibits in connection with Scripter.

Scripter evenings have been extremely successful in terms of their style and content, but uneven as fundraising events. When we have been successful in obtaining underwriting, we have raised as much as $70,000; when we have not, we have raised minimal amounts of money. Meanwhile, many of our supporters and members of the Friends board have fallen in love with the event. However, the fundraising team and university librarian that originally launched Scripter have since gone, and more recent players have not had a similar commitment to it.

Here, then, is an apt illustration of the uniqueness principle at work: the Scripter Award suited the style of one university librarian and his staff, but does not particularly suit the style of another university librarian and his staff. What worked well in one administration does not necessarily work well in another.

What has special collections gained by supporting Scripter? The event has provided an opportunity to cultivate and solicit a certain number of prospects but, apart from that, my department has, in fact, benefited very little. Indeed, it has expended more than it has gained. But direct accruals to special collections have never been the reason for participating in Scripter. Rather, as a member of the development team, my aim has been to support the overall fundraising goals of the library. Having been a development director, I know only too well how difficult and stressful large-scale fundraising events can be, and I certainly wanted to see our development program succeed on a large and public scale.

From the preceding remarks, the reader will gather that library fundraising is not an exact science. It is an art that depends on the talents, personalities, and styles of librarians and development officers, on the circumstances of the institutions for which they work, and on the unique factors at work in the communities in which those institutions are located. Everything connected with fundraising is subject to complex dynamics and inevitable change.

Nevertheless, if librarians and fundraisers follow some of the principles discussed here, their development program has, I believe, a far better chance of achieving and sustaining success than it would otherwise. If those involved in the fundraising process bear in mind the uniqueness and niche of their library and its collections, if the library director makes a sincere commitment to fundraising, and if the development director conscientiously serves as the director's guide, an ethical and vital effort can result. Last, if mutual trust, respect, and openness can be established among members of the development team, the group will have an excellent chance to meet and surmount the financial challenges facing all libraries today.

Note

Steele, Victoria and Stephen D. Elder. 1992. *Becoming a fundraiser: The principles and practice of library development*. Chicago: American Library Association.

Appendix

Library Fundraising Resource Center

The Library Fundraising Resource Center (LFRC) is a new source available to give comprehensive help to libraries in their efforts to design and implement fundraising plans. Increasingly, libraries are recognizing the critical importance of developing fundraising strategies in order to ensure their very survival.

Initiated as a two-year project funded, in part, by the W. K. Kellogg Foundation and the Carnegie Corporation of New York, LFRC's first undertaking is to offer fundraising training to librarians and trustees from sixty selected small and medium-sized libraries. In collaboration with the Fundraising School at the Indiana University Center on Philanthropy, four regional intensive three-day workshops are to be offered in seven fundamental technical areas of fundraising, with special focus on research and donor development, volunteer involvement, and strengthening governing boards.

Similar training programs are available through LFRC to other libraries. Participants are exposed to both theory and practice by exploring case studies in annual giving, major gifts solicitation and management, capital development, corporate and foundation partnerships, planned giving, special events management, and direct mail programs. Follow-up or on-site evaluation and consultation is also available for libraries that prefer this option.

The Resource Center also provides access to a broad spectrum of literature, including materials in these categories: case statements, capital campaigns, foundation proposals, corporate proposals, annual funds, special event programs, planned or deferred giving, strategic planning, records management, and donor recognition. A computerized database of national fundraising resources includes not only books, pamphlets, and other materials written for the library fundraiser, but also names of other libraries that have conducted successful campaigns and blueprints of how they attained their success.

Future plans include working on programs in fundraising to be offered at the American Library Association's annual conference, or as a special continuing education course in connection with graduate library schools across the nation. Additionally, the LFRC will continue to work with the Indiana University Center on Philanthropy to develop advanced training programs for library development professionals, library management, and governing boards.

For more information, contact: Library Fundraising Resource Center, American Library Association, 50 East Huron Street, Chicago, IL 60611. Phone: 312-280-5050, or 800-545-2433, ext. 5050.

Bibliography

Barsook, B. 1987. Is a retail business for you? In S. Dolnick, ed. *Fundraising for nonprofit institutions*. Greenwich, Conn.: JAI.

> This article concludes: "If you are considering opening a store, be serious about it from the beginning. Manage it like the business it is. Commit the funds necessary. . . ."

Burlingame, D. F. 1994. Fund-raising as a key to the library's future. *Library Trends* 42 (3): 467–77.

> The critical role of fundraising in articulating the library's mission is examined, underlining historical roots as well as contemporary issues in library development.

_____, ed. 1990. *Library development: A future imperative*. New York: Haworth.

> This volume covers the gamut of fundraising for libraries—from definitions of philanthropy to specific techniques for raising money, ending with a bibliography of works which delve further into these issues. The book blends theory and practice in a way that is useful for all involved in library development.

_____. 1990. Public libraries and fundraising: Not-so-strange bedfellows. *Library Journal* 115 (12): 52–54.

> The article summarizes a survey of 394 libraries and their use of fundraising to help defray expenses. The author concludes fundraising is important to libraries, both to help supplement tax dollars for operating costs and to enable libraries to offer new and innovative services.

Carrigan, D. P. Jan./Feb. 1994. Public library private fund-raising: A report based on a survey. *Public Libraries:* 31–36.

> Private fundraising by public libraries is increasingly important as tax dollars for libraries are cut. The experiences of some libraries successful in fundraising are reported.

Clark, C. S. 1992. Hard times for libraries. (issue theme) *CQ Researcher* 2 (24): 549–71.

The article presents a brief history and timeline of public libraries in the United States, ending with the drastic cuts in federal funding of libraries during the Reagan years. It highlights broad-based public support for funding of libraries.

D'Elia, G. and E. J. Rodger. Jan./Feb. 1994. Public opinion about the roles of the public library in the community: The results of a recent Gallup poll. *Public Libraries:* 23–28.

A national survey reports that the public considers the role of the library in supporting formal education to be the most important. Several other surveys of library users are reported.

Dewey, B. I., ed. 1991. *Raising money for academic and research libraries.* New York: Neal-Schuman.

This nuts-and-bolts, how-to book contains specific methods for raising money for libraries. The authors are successful library development officers who provide a broad spectrum of fundraising techniques to the reader.

Dolnick, S., ed. 1990. *Friends of libraries sourcebook.* Chicago: American Library Association.

A complete guide to the use of Friends of the Library groups, this book covers such general topics as voluntarism, fundraising, advocacy, and public relations as well as more specific topics such as literacy programs and computer literacy.

Goldberg, S. 1993. Fund raising, friend raising: The San Antonio Public Library foundation. *Bottom Line* 7 (1): 37–39.

The article offers helpful insights into the role of the library foundation in relationship to the management of the library.

Sirota, M. 1992. Time is money: Suggestions for more effective fundraising in the 1990s. *Bottom Line* 6 (1): 15–18.

This article highlights the effective use of research, cultivation techniques, and solicitation to produce the desired result. The steps in fundraising and the use of volunteers are also discussed.

Steele, V. and S. D. Elder. 1992. *Becoming a fundraiser: The principles and practice of library development.* Chicago: American Library Association.

The authors emphasize the critical role librarians play in fundraising for libraries. This work explores all aspects of library development in a practical and readable way.

Swan, J. 1990. *Fundraising for the small public library*. New York: Neal-Schuman.

   This "how-to-do-it" manual leads the reader through the various steps of fundraising on a relatively small scale.

Tucker, D. C. 1992. Donor research can improve your library's fundraising efforts. *Bottom Line* 6 (2): 17–22.

   Setting up a prospect research department in a library may be a somewhat complex task initially, but can more than pay for itself in the long run, as explained in this article.

Index